More than Meets the Eye

For Carrie —
the finest first
grade teacher.
— Donna

*E*ducation is understanding relationships.

—*George Washington Carver*

*A*nd now here is my secret, a very simple secret:
It is only with the heart that one can see rightly;
What is essential is invisible to the eye.

—*Antoine de Saint-Exúpery,* **The Little Prince**

More than Meets the Eye

HOW RELATIONSHIPS
ENHANCE LITERACY LEARNING

DONNA SKOLNICK

HEINEMANN
Portsmouth, NH

This book is dedicated to my parents—

To Esther Larsen Fellows Frederickson, my role model in teaching, courage, and love of learning and life.

And to Willard Winston Fellows (1913–1952), who I knew for seven short years, but lives on in my life.

D. S.

Heinemann
A division of Reed Elsevier Inc.
361 Hanover Street
Portsmouth, NH 03801–3912
www.heinemann.com

Offices and agents throughout the world

Library of Congress Cataloging-in-Publication Data
Skolnick, Donna.
    More than meets the eye : how relationships enhance literacy learning / Donna Skolnick.
        p. cm.
    Includes bibliographical references.
    ISBN 0-325-00249-5 (alk. paper)
    1. Language arts (Elementary).   2. Reading (Elementary).   3. English language—Composition and exercises—Study and teaching (Elementary).   4. Teacher-student relationships.   I. Title.
    LB1576. S575   2000
    372.6—dc21

                                                                                        00-039524

Editor: William Varner
Production: Abigail M. Heim
Cover design: Joni Doherty Design
Manufacturing: Deanna Richardson

Printed in the United States of America on acid-free paper

04   03   02   01   00   DA   1   2   3   4   5

Contents

Foreword

RALPH FLETCHER

*R*elationships. I'm convinced that's what draws individuals to the teaching profession—the thrill and challenge of engaging with human beings in the spring of their lives, and deepening their understanding of the world.

Today, in the current frenzy of proficiency tests, that fundamental pleasure has become an endangered species. We have seen the commodification of learning in which programs claim as a selling point (!) to be "teacher-proof." What a ringing vote of confidence! More and more, teachers feel as if they are being required to help their kids jump through test hoops. The debate continues to rage over tests, but one thing is certain—that's not what brought these people into teaching in the first place.

Maybe that's why I found Donna Skolnick's new book, *More than Meets the Eye: How Relationships Enhance Literacy Learning*, so refreshing. Donna's book is a ringing reminder that teachers and kids, and the interplay between them, reside at the core of education.

While I was halfway through this manuscript my wife and coauthor, JoAnn Portalupi, asked me about Donna's book. "Is it practical or visionary?" she wanted to know.

"Yes," I replied, meaning *both*. New teachers will revel in the specific teaching strategies for bringing students to the meeting area, letting students sketch or draw on scrap paper during read alouds. When it comes to the nuts and bolts of teaching second and third grade children, Donna Skolnick has forgotten more than most of us will ever know.

But the book does not stop there. She brings the reader into her vision of classroom learning in the language arts. She explores the difference between transactional and transformational relationships.

Donna's book is grounded in her own professional experience as well as her own journey as a reader/writer. While she draws on many eclectic sources—Daniel Goleman, Howard Gardner, Leslie Hart, Eric Jensen, Vivian Paley—Donna's own strong voice runs like a river through these pages. I found something wonderful on almost every page. Often I had to stop so I could underline or copy a pithy passage. This is a book to sip, to savor. In passage after thoughtful passage, the author reminds us of the myriad ways teachers affect the lives of children:

> In many ways, the *who* we are as teachers is an unacknowledged curriculum. Our values and beliefs come through our every action in subtle and unexpected ways. How we perceive the curriculum and our relationship to it cannot be filtered out of our daily school lives. Even children who cannot read can read between the lines.

Donna knows her material very well, and presents it in lively, often quotable prose: "Watching their teacher think out loud, children learn about the backstage of literacy. It's as eye-opening as a backstage pass."

She writes: "When children are upset, they often slip into global language, too. 'Everybody hates me' or 'Nobody will play with me' on closer inspection means that one or two children will not play or are angry with them."

At another point, she makes a revealing distinction between accepting and tolerating the behavior of children. I found nuggets like these nourishing not just for my teaching but for my parenting as well.

READ THIS BOOK. READ IT WITH HIGHLIGHTER IN HAND, OR JUST sit back and savor the pages. As I read I became aware of all the experience behind each word. Here is the wisdom of a teacher who has worked with kids for thirty years, but has never lost track of the inherent thrill. This is an important book full of compassion, humor, and wisdom. At one point she writes: "When the teacher reads and writes with the class, it is like yeast to bread dough. All are elevated."

I have no doubt that all teachers, whether new or experienced, will be as elevated as I was by Donna Skolnick's buoyant, yeasty book.

Acknowledgments

*W*riting this book reminds me of Jack and the Beanstalk. I knew what I wanted to say and expected the writing to be a rather straightforward process. Like Jack's ungainly beanstalk, the seeds of my ideas grew far beyond my original plan. My mind filled with huge overgrown ideas that twisted and wound back and forth, extending my horizon. The imagined book, quick and easy to write, turned into a lengthy journey of learning and self-discovery.

Along the way, I had family, friends, and colleagues who gave me encouragement to continue the climb.

Thank you to my family. When Sara or Scott asked, "How's it going, Mom?" I felt their commitment to the book and their support of my prolonged project. They have taught me about relationships and seeing through the eyes of love. My husband, Harv, continues to be my number one fan, bringing home dinners and nourishing my spirit as well. His positive energy has been a powerful force in my life. Thank you, kind sir.

My four special sisters encouraged me with their confidence that I had something important to write. Our conversations on the phone and email left me smiling and recharged. I'm so glad we have outgrown our annoying behaviors of childhood and have become such wise and loving friends. Thank you Nancy, Karen, Suzanne, and Betty.

My years as a teacher in Westport, Connecticut, have been filled with wonderful relationships. Thank you to the highly professional and caring teachers at Coleytown Elementary School. It was a pleasure to join you each day in our most important endeavor. And to my new friends and colleagues at Kings Highway School—your dedication, creativity, and belief in children radiates in all you do.

Thank you to Mary Winsky and Judy Luster. Your company around my dining room table on Friday afternoons brings a special sparkle to my life. You never fail to teach me something I need to learn as we tell our stories, recommend books, laugh, and write together.

A big hug to Nancy Kovacic and Michele Cunningham. You know how much you have added to my life in the past few years. When I'm with you I'm guaranteed lots of laughter and lots of big ideas to ponder. Keep leading the way.

Thank you to my assistant superintendent, Lynne Shain, and the other curriculum resource teachers, Caltha Crowe, Karen Emanuelson, and Karen Ernst daSilva. Your deep thinking about challenging educational issues is an inspiration. I am in such capable and committed company.

Jane Fraser, my coauthor for *On Their Way: Celebrating Second Graders as They Read and Write,* patiently read through the rough drafts of the manuscript and offered thoughtful revisions. I am indebted to you, Jane, for your wise counsel and valued friendship.

Thank you to my dear friend, Anne Nesbitt, who believed that I could write a book of consequence. Her rare ability to conceptualize ideas in fresh ways is a continual delight. So many thanks, Anne.

Many treasured friends encouraged me to continue climbing the beanstalk, but the extensive root system began its growth with mentors back in the 1980s. They provided the foundation for much of the work I do with children. A big thank-you to Lucy Calkins, Don Graves, Nancie Atwell, and Mary Ellen Giocobbe. Like so many teachers and children across the country, I am grateful for your groundbreaking work with reading and writing workshop. How fortunate I am to be able to learn with you.

Bill Varner at Heinemann has been the perfect editor for me. When I needed space to linger and write, he was patient and supportive. When I needed nudging, he kindly but clearly helped me stick to a timetable. His suggestions for revisions hit the mark every time. Thank you, Bill. You made my first solo book a great experience. And thank you, Abby Heim, for your careful supervision of the manuscript once it went into production. I appreciate your patient guidance.

To the hundreds, perhaps thousands, of children who've shared my daily life—I send you my love and my thanks. Never lose your wonder at the world. I embrace each of you as the ordinary miracles you are.

1

The Role of Relationships in Literacy Learning

Relationships reside at the heart of lasting stories: Wilbur and Charlotte, Dorothy and the Wicked Witch, Cinderella and Prince Charming. Relationships transform characters, sending some to their fortunes, some to their demise. Like the roots of a sturdy old oak, relationships anchor literary characters and give them their texture and definition.

Relationships are just as powerful and transforming in the classroom. They sustain or deplete the learning community. That's what this book is about—the crucial role of relationships in our daily school lives. To understand the subtle but deciding differences that influence the learning landscape in each classroom, we must see the relationships that weave together the community of learners.

If you peek into several elementary classrooms, they look fairly similar. You'll see desks, student work and posters on the walls, maybe colorful pictures hanging like wash on a line. Students may be quietly at work, heads bent over books or papers, or talking with each other in small groups around the room. The scenes will look basically the same and yet the learning environment in each room can vary dramatically.

As a townwide writing teacher in many classrooms from 1984 to 1989, I was intrigued that one classroom hummed with productivity and enthusiasm and the one right next door sagged with the weight of the work. Both rooms had teachers committed to the children and the curriculum, working hard to do their best. From outward appearances, it was difficult to tell why one setting was robust and one was lackluster.

Then as a teacher researcher with Lucy Calkins at Teachers College, I read *The Culture of the School and the Problem of Change* (Sarason 1982). When Sarason mentioned the critical role of relationships in the classroom,

1

a bell pinged in my brain. As I began to study classroom interaction at this deeper level, I saw past the children at work to the more illusive picture—the relationships that shape the learning landscape. These relationships are

- between teacher and student
- between and among students
- between teacher and curriculum
- between student and curriculum

This book focuses specifically on the curriculum areas of reading and writing. These acts of literacy are the most important subjects taught in schools, for they make learning the other disciplines possible. We have learned so much in the past two decades about how children acquire language and the ability to read and write. Ever-increasing information about brain function, multiple intelligences, learning styles and preferences have contributed to our understanding of how to support young readers and writers. It is my firm conviction that relationships add another necessary piece to the puzzle.

When I returned to classroom teaching ten years ago from my townwide position, I continued to test my theory that relationships shape and define the learning environment. Extensive conversations with colleagues furthered my convictions. Beneath the obvious concerns of daily classroom life lies the network that can transform it into a place where joyfully literate children practice the habits of lifelong readers and writers.

My beliefs have grown into *knowing*. I *know* that how I nurture the key relationships in my classroom determines the nature of our time together. Resilient relationships maximize our individual and group potential. Weakened relationships inhibit harmony, creativity, and achievement.

In *Emotional Intelligence*, Daniel Goleman describes this phenomenon in terms of group IQ, the collective ability of a group to function well and create positive outcomes. "It is this ability to harmonize that, all other things being equal, will make one group especially talented, productive, and successful and another—with members whose talent and skill are equal in other regards—do poorly" (1995, 160). When the primary relationships in the classroom receive proper care and attention, the collective IQ soars.

Several years ago I stood at the mall with my daughter Sara. It was our first time seeing magic eye pictures. There were ten or twelve large pictures and at least that many people bobbing back and forth, in and out, trying to see the picture hidden behind geometric patterns.

"I see it!" an excited boy told his father. "Look, it's a flying dragon!"

His dad moved around and shook his head. "Wait . . . I think I've got it."

I looked at Sara and shrugged. She shrugged back. Was there really another picture embedded in the obvious one? It felt like a trick. Maybe we were on *Candid Camera* and everyone else was just pretending to see another picture. We moved on down the mall.

Neither of us saw a hidden picture that day, nor were we even convinced that there was one. Several months later I decided to try again. This time the large picture was framed and behind glass. Eureka! I could see the hidden picture! I had to dodge around, but eventually the invisible picture came into focus. What a sense of satisfaction I felt!

I love those magic eye pictures for the metaphor they offer about life in the elementary classroom. To truly understand the invisible forces behind a classroom of busy children, we must see beyond the surface of the picture and let other shapes and patterns emerge. We begin to see that it is these interrelationships that control behavior and determine daily patterns of teaching and learning. A caring, adaptive teacher with clear classroom expectations, the way children talk with and listen to each other, and structures that support their work as readers and writers—these meld together to decide the way life is lived.

A sense of membership—that deep basic human need—provides one measure of relationships. Students who have strong connections to other children in the class feel they belong. They're part of the group—insiders. When they have a strong connection to their reading and writing, they belong to the literacy club. Even at an emergent level, they read, write, and join in conversations about books and writing. They are readers and writers among many, expanding their literacy horizons together. Another group is the teacher's pet club, in which absolutely every child has a guaranteed membership—if their name is on the class roster, they're automatically a member. One benefit of membership in this club is that the teacher will not give up until he has found each child's strengths. Then he slowly and purposefully begins to build on them. When children believe they belong to these classroom clubs, flourishing relationships cradle them with an aura of distinction and pride.

For the purposes of this book, I am viewing relationships as two primary kinds: *transactional* and *transformational*. They exist side by side in classrooms. Transactional and transformational relationships occur each and every day and are a necessary part of classroom life. Although transactional interactions dominate in classrooms, it is transformational relationships that I focus on. A closer look at each type of relationship will explain why.

Transactional Relationships. These relationships make the world go 'round. Without these functional relationships, life on the planet would come to a screeching halt. Most conversations and discussions in school are transactional. Their purpose is to get things done, to complete a transaction. For example, it is time for reading; the second-grade teacher wants the class to complete a specific assignment in their reading response journals. She explains the tasks and the children get to work. The class runs smoothly, the children know what to do and also what to do when they finish the assignment. The personal engagement with the teacher is based on conversations about the task at hand.

These relationships can be warm, supportive, and caring, but their focus is short-term and on the transaction to be completed. There is a mutual respect and the expectation that both sides of the transaction are doing their part. Difficulty arises when one side of the equation falters or does not deliver the expected results. Kids in the classroom who cannot deliver the learning goods strain the transaction. The teacher feels like the salesperson who dragged out fifteen pairs of shoes and the customer walked away unshod. A transactional relationship is especially susceptible to frustration and disappointment.

Remember the old traditional classrooms where the teacher supposedly used the same lesson plans year after year? It didn't matter who was in the class, what they knew, or what they needed to learn. If the class finished page fifty-five yesterday, they did page fifty-six today. The relationships were purely transactional. The teacher cared about her class and cared about covering the curriculum, but little varied from day to day, year to year. Children marched through the room to the same drumbeat regardless of the rhythm of the group or the individual rhythms of each child.

A friend of mine recently described the marriage of her parents: "They have a life together but no relationship." Aha! I thought. That can happen in a classroom, too. In our busy lives together, we complete tasks and move along with the swift current, but we never truly connect to each other or to the learning that needs to take place.

A transactional relationship is

- based on the task to be completed
- focused on the short-term
- warm and caring at times
- over when the transaction is complete

Transformational Relationships. These relationships are founded in mutual knowledge and understanding. They allow us to be transformed as we learn and grow. Participants are influenced by and responsive to each other. Like the slender reed in Aesop's fable, transformational relationships are flexible and resilient. They can survive the storm and still be intact when the dark clouds pass. Ideally, the relationship is neither controlling nor confining and there is a sense that we are appreciated and accepted for who we are. We trust that we are doing our best, even if our best is not always that good.

What changes a transactional relationship into a transformational one? I believe it's *listening softly*. Active and fully engaged listening allows trust and respect to blossom as we deeply hear the words and ideas of others. Richard Carlson and Joseph Bailey, in *Slowing Down to the Speed of Life* (1997), describe it this way: "True listening allows you to change your mind. It allows you to see something fresh, in a new way. It enables you to say to others or to yourself, 'I've never thought of that before.' It's the kind of listening that creates enjoyment and a sharp learning curve" (59).

My five years as the townwide writing teacher gave me practice in softly listening to young writers. When writer's block struck, I studied their eyes as we talked. Suddenly a flash of energy would flicker, and I knew we had hit pay dirt. As I watched for their internal energy to reignite, I trusted my open-minded listening to kindle the flame. Time and again, my focused listening sparked their ideas. The more I listened, the more I realized its power.

Sometimes, to keep the classroom momentum, I try to listen too fast. I become Teflon-coated, letting the words of students wash over me rather than penetrate my thoughts. When I permit the pressures of time to invade the classroom, listening is lost. Transactional interactions must suffice.

Life in the classroom where transformational relationships flourish may look similar to life next door in the predominantly transactional classroom, but the ambience and results are different. Transformational relationships have deep roots that have been propagated and nurtured. They are living and organic connections that permit a continuous and spontaneous exchange of energy and information. The reciprocity of the connections enhances and enlarges both sides of the learning equation. These are win-win relationships where both teacher and student feel successful and privileged in their intensely collaborative projects.

Structures and rituals in the transformational classroom permit different and varied rhythms, so it must be just as systematic and organized as a primarily transactional classroom. In these responsive settings, where the teacher is influenced by the students and vice versa, she relies on a range of repertoires that match the needs and learning styles.

A transformational relationship is

- reciprocal— influencing each other
- based on understanding and trust

- supportive and nourishing
- shared concern for each other

Although I spoke earlier of the four relationships as though they were separate entities, please imagine these relationships as an interconnected whole. See the delicate way they weave together and the intricate lacework they create. By looking at the classroom through the lens of relationships, there is an openness necessary to unearth the shortcomings in our usual way of viewing classroom life. Focusing on and studying classroom relationships creates a flexibility and responsiveness not available when our emphasis is primarily on children and curriculum as though they were distinct and disconnected.

We gain a fresh vantage point when we view the classroom as an operating system connected by relationships. Embracing the system rather than the individual parts allows us to search for new potentials. Like the magic eye pictures, the obvious dissolves, revealing a totally new vista.

In *The Fifth Discipline: The Art and Practice of the Learning Organization*, Peter Senge focuses on systems thinking. "Systems thinking . . . is a framework for seeing interrelationships rather than things . . . a sensibility for the subtle interconnectedness that gives living systems their unique character" (1990, 69). And who would deny the unique character of every class? It is why last year's lesson plan doesn't fit the new class any better than their last year's shoes.

Of course, a disclaimer is in order. As a classroom teacher, I don't want to give the impression that each year I orchestrate the perfect classroom. I have not found a way to create Stepford Kids, although there are days it sounds appealing. No—I am a real teacher with real students. And as the Greek philosopher Heraclitus said, "You cannot step into the same river twice for fresh waters are ever flowing in." I know I never step into the same classroom twice. The flow of the classroom river is rapid and constant. Each day children bring new sets of concerns, interests, curiosities, and experiences. It is not my goal to shape my students into manageable packages through manipulating relationships. My intention each day and each year is to pay attention to the four vital relationships so I can help the children be full participants in their own learning and in the group. In this way, they can discover their identities as readers, writers, and learners.

This deeper focus also gives me greater clarity of direction. It helps me avoid getting caught in the thick of *thin* things. Understanding the key role of relationships and how they impact our time together guides me when the waters get rough. While trying to stay in the here and now as I work with each student, I am also charting against my long-term goals just as the North Star guided the early sailors. Always in my mind is the question, "Will the decisions I am making help these children become lifelong learners, lifelong readers and writers—adults who will be comfortable and contributing members of our society?" These goals can feel weighty at times and get lost in the frantic cha-cha of the classroom dance. But my focus on relationships pulls me back to my guiding question. I can't settle for anything less. Nor do I want those of us who live our lives among children to want anything less for them.

Research shows that teachers make at least two thousand decisions a day (Saphier and Gower 1987). With that rapid pace, we need a touchstone for easy reference. Relationships provide that touchstone. For example, my class is settling in to sustained silent reading. Quiet is replacing the hustle and bustle as children find their books, make one final comment to a friend, and squeak their chairs into a comfortable position. Sarah appears at my side. "May Briana and I read to each other out in the hall? We're on the same chapter of *Fantastic Mr. Fox*."

My "yes" to Sarah and Briana could be based on expediency or a "why not?" attitude, but it runs deeper than that. I want to promote their love of Roald Dahl's delightful story *and* their friendship. Their relationship to their reading and to each other are both fostered by the time they spend together with the clever Mr. Fox. The expectations for working in the hall are clear and I trust the girls to use their time well. When my guiding principle is strengthening relationships—not just child to child, but child to reading and writing—the appropriate decision requires less energy. Saying "yes" in this particular instance was a win-win for all of us—teacher, students, and clever Mr. Fox.

After a number of years of contemplating how relationships shape and enrich my classroom practice, I trust the decisions I make based on that focus. My concern and affection for the children, their respect for each other, and our positive attitude toward reading and writing stand us in good stead in our daily lives. The myriad of decisions I make in the course of a day is streamlined as I measure them against the unwavering central focus of relationships. The energy I save by not deliberating over every decision flows back into and strengthens the relationships. When I am totally there—in the moment—trusting what I do, trusting the children as learners, trusting the power of language and story to reel them in, all's right with the world. Not all moments can be like that, but they are more frequent and possible when the classroom relationships are healthy and vital.

As I write this book, I hope that I can help you see the fascinating web of relationships that define the classroom environment and how paying attention to and strengthening them will improve the quality of reading and writing life in your classroom. The chapters focus on one relationship at a time, explaining its significance with classroom examples. A second chapter about each relationship offers suggestions for practical ways to build those relationships. They focus on ways teachers and students can live each classroom day fully awake and alive, engaged in effective and enduring work.

Building and strengthening relationships means living our classroom lives by design, not by default. It means considering more than our own needs and desires. When the priority is forging connections in the classroom, our query shifts from "What do I want to cover in the curriculum?" to more complex questions:

- How can I foster a lifelong relationship between my students and their reading and writing?
- How can I help my students live meaningful lives in our classroom community?
- How can I value and learn from each child?

These are more demanding questions than "What are the learning objectives of this lesson?" or "What do I want the students to know and do?" Looking at relationships casts our vision further down the road. It means looking ahead and fixing on a more distant and profound goal. The transactions of the classroom become weightier and more purposeful. This is not just for today. This is not about getting it done. This is about making lasting connections that students will need in the twenty-first century—that we all need every day in our lives.

As you read about my classroom and those of my colleagues, please think of this as an invitation to reflect on your own classroom. Pull back and become the observer of *your* domain. What do you notice about the relationships? What are the values and assumptions that govern your teaching practices? These are big questions. In the fast pace of today's schools we don't often have time to take a deep breath or have a complete thought, let alone pause to reflect. But it's imperative that we do. It is my fondest dream that this book add greater clarity to your perception of classroom dynamics. Even if you reject all my suggestions for making stronger connections but gain a better understanding of why you do what you do, you, too, may glimpse the enchanting picture that lies beyond our traditional focus.

2

The Relationship Between the Teacher and the Student

or adults who do not spend their days with children, it's easy to confuse a child's smaller stature with smaller concerns and smaller cares. But children are just as complex and as complicated as adults. They arrive at school each morning with their own elaborate world of needs, issues, and ideas. For the classroom to run smoothly and productively, each student needs a strong connection to the teacher. Just as spokes on a wheel connect to the hub, the connection between the child and the teacher needs to be secure as the class rolls through its busy day. A broken spoke or two, and the wheel begins to wobble. Building a healthy and vital connection to each child creates a sense of security and possibility. Then the bike can leave the track and roam the highways and byways. Solid relationships maximize learning and personal growth.

THE GREATER MY INFLUENCE, THE SMOOTHER THE RIDE. . . .

When my class sits in the circle to start our day together, I skim the sea of eager faces: Diana, Lisa, Michael, Jared. As we hold hands and pass the electricity squeeze each Friday morning, I smile at our togetherness. I know that my influence with the class is no stronger than my relationship with each child. A sturdy connection to each one ensures a durable relationship with the group as a whole. We support and care about each other and that sense must radiate from the center of the spoke—the teacher. The greater my influence, the smoother the ride for all of us. Early in the year as I am learning about each child and initiating the relationships, some days feel like a ride on the old-fashioned boneshaker bicycle. We bounce with every bump in the road and it's not easy to steer around potholes. But as the weeks pass and I know the children better, our daily ride is less laborious. We've traded the boneshaker for a shiny new touring mountain bike, complete with gears. When my relationships with the children are firmly established on trust and respect, learning goes up and classroom management issues go down.

Jessica had a continual power struggle with her first-grade teacher, and spent many afternoons at the principal's office. As I came to understand Jessica's needs and personality in second grade, I realized that a power struggle would be a lose-lose situation. Many a morning I tried to connect to Jessica the minute she walked through the door. I needed her on my side and I wanted to be on hers. With the help of the school psychologist, I figured out strategies for helping Jessica be a good class member. There were days it took fancy footwork and an intense focus on what she did right, but the effort was worth it.

Some children, like Jessica, come to school with private issues that make it difficult for them to be a good group member. Others are ready and eager to contribute to the group. Still others are more passive, but willing to follow along. A caring and strong relationship with each child strengthens the entire group. The old adage "A chain is no stronger than its weakest link" also holds true for the classroom. Working on those weak links—developing caring and genuine affection for the children who need our help to be contributing class members—means our energy can go into teaching and learning, not crowd control.

Positive relationships have a continual flow of energy. Information moves back and forth and insures the vitality of the relationship. The spoke supports the hub and the hub supports the spokes. The teacher is there to help each student learn and grow. The students help the teacher through their thoughtful work and cooperation. The relationship is interdependent. For many years the relationship between teacher and student was considered to be more like the power plant, with energy flowing one way—from the teacher to the student. But a closer look at a vigorous classroom and the bicycle wheel emerges. The relationships are reciprocal and responsive.

In *The Power Principle: Influence with Honor,* Blaine Lee describes the benefits of relationships founded on honor and respect, rather than coercion and control. "It invites synergy, in which the contributions of all parties combine to create new options and new opportunities greater than—better than—anything you could do or be on your own" (101). Later, he quotes a teacher as saying, " I believe that we can accelerate learning for all students, especially at-risk students, by building relationships" (236).

SEE MORE IN A CHILD
THAN SHE SEES IN HERSELF

This past summer I was surprised to run into a former student at the beach. She's now a thirty-eight-year-old mother of a four-year-old sand castle builder. She looked much the same as she had in fourth grade, and she tried to convince me that I, too, was unchanged. I easily recalled getting to know her almost thirty years earlier. Not all children are so memorable, but her name was also Donna and I remember how she came to fourth grade expecting me not to like her. That made me, the young invincible teacher, determined that I *would* like her—and I did! I remember discovering a side to her that she had decided was safer to hide. She trusted me enough to let me see the softer, gentler, more needy side that she had been protecting.

As we stood in the warm summer sun laughing about all the time that had passed, she remarked, "You're the only teacher I remember from elementary school."

"It's because we're both named Donna," I joked.

"No," she insisted. "You were the only one who believed in me. You saw who I really was."

I walked across the sand on hot, winged feet. What a precious gift she had just given me.

I stored Donna's words away. The new school year was approaching and I resolved to make a difference for the kids who would soon be crowding through the classroom door. But that's what summer is for—the renewal of spirit and resolve. In my best and strongest summer moments, I am confident that I can believe in every child.

Don Murray said it so well, speaking at a conference at the University of New Hampshire: "My job is to see more in my students than they see in themselves." What inspirational words—they capture in a simple phrase the kind of teacher I want to be. How fortunate for me that I had teachers like that when I was in elementary school all those years ago. And I am luckier than the Donna I had for fourth grade. I remember all of my elementary teachers. Each gave me a sense that I was somehow special.

It was Mrs. Howe in first grade who convinced me to be a teacher. I didn't need to make a career decision at six, but I was ready to join the teaching staff of Washington Elementary School. I wanted to have the same perfect printing, the same smooth bun, the same gentle power. And she believed in me. She chose me to be the narrator in our class play, *Goldilocks and the Three Bears*. Granted, I did have bouncy blond curls like Goldilocks, but it was an honor to be the narrator. I had the most lines. The second daughter in a family of five girls, I was a spunky little show-off, but Mrs. Howe liked me anyway.

The summer before second grade, my father died suddenly. My mother returned to teaching in the fall and I changed schools so the three of us who were of school age could ride with her to school. Mrs. Finkbinder, my generous and caring second grade teacher, helped me to feel capable and special. Whether she felt sorry for me because I had just lost my father, or whether I *was* as precocious as she made me feel, it was a time in my life when I needed an ego boost and some TLC. I carry Mrs. Finkbinder in my heart and as an adult I understand what she did for me. Our relationship gave me the helping heart I needed as a stunned seven-year-old.

EVERY CHILD DESERVES TO BE LIKED

All children have their own particular needs, some greater than others. There are days when meeting all the needs seems daunting, but I know the effort makes a difference in the life of a child. And the flip side is just as true— watching a child make the small steps or the big leap is good for me, too. It's why I set my alarm each evening, even though I may forget the exact reason when it blares in the predawn darkness.

I would have done anything for Mrs. Howe and Mrs. Finkbinder and the rest of my elementary teachers. They had tremendous influence with me because they gave me a sense that I was a capable and lovable little kid. The IALAC concept (I Am Lovable And Capable) from the early days of values clarification makes even more sense in light of recent research into brain function. When we feel lovable and capable, our ability to learn is enhanced. Priscilla Vail calls emotions our "on/off switch for learning" (1994). Children who do not have an emotionally clear channel cannot learn with the same enthusiasm and pace. The static on their learning channel interferes with their ability to take in new information or apply what they already know.

Children possess strong built-in sensors to detect how adults feel about them. Even a sweet sounding teacher, if he happens to dislike a student, sends off alarm bells. Those bells should not toll for any child. Liking every child in our class is not a right—it is a privilege, and sometimes an effort. But it is our job. When I say *like,* I don't mean we wish to adopt them and bring them home, although some children each year would fit into that category. By *like,* I mean that we respect and honor who they are. We know them well, inside and out, upside down, and sideways.

We are the ones who must initiate the relationship and start the positive feedback loop. Not all children are equally likable and appealing. But each year the children who take the most effort to get to know and appreciate are the children who teach us the most and push us to become better teachers. Children arrive that first day as if from central casting. The one who gets on our nerves is the one who needs our patience and understanding the most—the occasional child who just seems to push the wrong buttons. Her voice, attitude, or some elusive quality radiates out and plucks at our negativity. When I find that happening, I know I have to go into overdrive to find ways to truly like and appreciate that child.

ACT YOUR WAY INTO FEELING

As the hoard of young strangers enter our rooms each fall, we may not feel immediate fondness for all of them, but of course, we act as if we do. By acting as though we feel affection—bestowing our best listening, patience, and kindness—we act our way into those feelings. Actions form feelings as letters form words. *Like* is a verb, an action word. When we act caring, we become caring. "*Act Loving and You'll Feel Loving* sounds like a bad song from the 70s," says an article entitled "How to Short-Circuit Negativity" in *Prevention* magazine, "but it's actually a smart thing to do . . . it can help stop negativity. Acting 'as if' is not denial or deception, but a deliberate effort to change the situation" (1997, 28).

In some cases, we bond very quickly with a child. Something in their smile, their manner, their apprehensive look resounds within us and we feel a warm and immediate connection. These kids bring out the best in us. Then there are those who don't. Personality conflicts, annoying habits, or misunderstandings about who's in charge damage the connection like faulty wiring. Whatever the reason, "fake it 'til you make it" is still the best advice.

The art of teaching can demand some Oscar-winning performances. As I am acting as though there is nothing I would rather do than help Paul find his fourteenth lost pencil, I am also trying to figure out how to help him solve his pencil problem. Still another part of my brain is curious to understand what makes it so hard for Paul to keep track of his things. Is this developmental? Is he overly anxious and therefore more distractible? Does he eat pencils? By helping Paul, I open up my heart to him and soon my acting becomes genuine affection.

One-on-one time away from the group helps me connect to a child more easily. Often children who appear cold and distant in a group setting are dramatically different in a solo part. We may have lunch together in the room, or clean the hamster cage at recess, organize the bookcase, collate and staple papers. When we're involved in an activity together, conversations flow naturally, at first around the work we're doing and then into personal anecdotes. Alone time means I can listen to their stories and share my own. Affection grows one story at a time. I search for similarities between us and find ways to share a smile. Stories and smiles connect our lives and invite us to care about each other.

Learning to like some children takes time and determination, but it can never be an option. Each day feels so much brighter when shared with children we enjoy. Both teacher and student win when they belong to the mutual admiration society.

At our conference last fall, Caroline's mother told me about her daughter's previous year in second grade. "The teacher didn't like her," she reported.

"Why did Caroline think that?" I asked. I wanted to find out if Caroline's gentle personality had changed along with her school.

"Well," her mother told me, "Caroline felt invisible. The teacher rarely called on her when she raised her hand. Caroline just felt she liked the other children better."

In a busy classroom it's easy to overlook some kids some days and a child's perception of classroom events may vary tremendously from the teacher's. Caroline's teacher probably had no idea how Caroline perceived their relationship. Of course, this young girl did not enjoy going to school and her learning curve hit a slump.

IT IS OUR JOB TO BE LIKABLE

Liking each child is only half of the equation. We must also *be* likable. I have yet to meet a young student who loved school, who loved to learn, who did not also love his teacher. Just like the chalk, eraser, and chalkboard, it's a package deal. Having a likable teacher does not guarantee a productive and worthwhile year in school, but the inverse *is* true. Without a likable teacher, the year *cannot* be productive and worthwhile for the student. Have you even known young children who felt positively about school who did not think their teachers were the best? These rare little birds may exist, but I'll wager they have unusual personalities and strength of character. Most children who step down from the big yellow bus in the morning want to be greeted in their classroom by someone they care about and like and someone who cares about and enjoys being with them.

In *The Skillful Teacher* (1987), Jon Saphier and Robert Gower write of a research study that interviewed students to find out what traits and behaviors in a teacher were most important to them. These traits "foster more personal regard for a teacher, which can be a basis of good personal relationships: fairness, appearance, humor, courtesy, respect, realness, reestablishing contact, active listening" (71). These seem like good guidelines to keep in mind. No one told me back in my education courses that I should be likeable as a teacher—no doubt my own need for center stage pushed me to win student approval back then. My reason may have been wrong, but my outcome was right. Children who admire their teacher bring a readiness and willingness to school along with the crumpled papers in their backpack.

KIDS AS CARS

Recently while driving to school, I conceived of a rather unusual way to help me accept each child for who he or she is: I imagined each child as a car. Every morning these individualized vehicles cruise through the door. Here are a few examples:

- David arrives. He is a solid model, no dents, no frills, but attractive and reliable. I know he'll get more than 100,000 miles of smooth travel and require little maintenance. An oil change or minimal attention periodically and he will zoom down life's highway, engine purring.

- Cody, on the other hand, chugs into the room sideswiping other cars as he proceeds to the closet to hang up his jacket. He is a large Cadillac from the seventies with big fins and lots of chrome. You don't want to park next to Cody in a parking lot. His car door will swing wide open, leaving a little chink or dent on your car. Sitting next to Cody in the circle is much the same—it's almost impossible to know where his elbow might land. His sensory integration system doesn't give him the information he needs about what his body is doing. His big steel fins can poke your own unprotected bumper at any moment. Some days, after ingesting the wrong fuel, his exhaust system emits unpleasant sounds and odors.

- Katie glides through the door, a small, snappy, sports convertible. With the top down, she can hear the latest news and contribute her tidbits. She zips around the room, stopping by each table to gossip and hear the latest. A high-powered vehicle, she is happiest in motion. Sometimes she darts between other cars too quickly, leaving chaos in her wake. When other children honk their horns or flash their lights, she asks, "What did I do?"

- Next comes Megan. The forlorn look on her face suggests her engine needs tuning or maybe a tire is flat. Her shock absorbers seem to have lost their spring and she will require major repair to help her through the day. It may be a bad day for her asthma or maybe the circles under her eyes are from a bad night's sleep. The light on her dashboard frequently flashes, *please seek assistance for service*. And she will.

- Will arrives as a small compact. His engine runs quietly and he rarely needs to be serviced. He gets excellent gas mileage, but he can't maintain the speed necessary for long distances. He chugs along in the slow lane, unconcerned by the cars passing by. Sometimes the road narrows into two lanes and a number of cars get backed up behind him as he slowly navigates hills at his own steady pace. His car will make it safely to the destination, but in its own good time.

By looking at the children in my class as cars, it lightens my mood and helps me to think more carefully about each one. It's a silly mental game, but when I look at Cody and think *seventies Cadillac,* I am able to see him from a fresh perspective. I gain the necessary distance to appreciate who children are and not want to change them into a make and model that would better suit my teaching style. I cannot make Cody's Cadillac into Will's small compact. I cannot whisk Megan into the repair shop for a magical tune-up so she will immediately have the stamina for a smoother, more independent ride.

Pretending children are cars also helps me to not take their behaviors personally. With the whirlwind pace each day, it is easy to feel unwanted student behavior as a personal affront. When I am rested and rational, I can see that the problem lies with the child and his needs in that moment. Cody is not thumping into his place in the circle to personally annoy me. His dated Cadillac just requires lots of space to maneuver. It's not about bugging the teacher at the end of a tiring day. At this point in time, this is who Cody is and he is doing the best he can. And unlike cars, these young vehicles develop and change.

WE ALL DO THE BEST WE CAN

Mary Ellen Giacobbe taught me this concept in a workshop the summer of 1984 on Martha's Vineyard. As she and Nancie Atwell talked to us about helping young writers, I copied down those thought-provoking words: *We all do the best we can.* Was this true? The words played in my head like a melody. I began by examining my own behavior. There are times when my best is not very good. But in that moment, it unfortunately *is* my best. When I'm tired and drained, stressed and feeling fragile, my best ain't very grand. But if I were capable of better in that situation, I would do it. Given the context and the history, in each moment we do the best we can.

I've mulled that idea over and over, observed how it played out in hundreds of situations, and I've decided it makes sense. It makes working with a classroom of children feel so much better, too. It doesn't mean that I accept any behavior or that I don't have high expectations or standards. Not at all.

But it does mean that when Megan is feeling vulnerable and needy, I trust her feelings and know that she would rather be spirited and joyful, as she is at other times. I accept her as she is in that moment and help her to be the best she can be, knowing that when she gives less of herself than I would like, it's her best right then in that context. The better I know her, the more strategies I'll have for helping her regain her equilibrium.

AN ADVOCATE FOR EACH CHILD

At the end of September, as I marked the attendance sheet, I mentioned that Martin was in Boston for a long weekend. The circle erupted with comments: "Yes! Martin's absent! Good news!" Did the class really find Martin so bothersome? I put down my pen and clipboard. Attendance and lunch count could wait. We needed to talk about this. I didn't want to focus on Martin, but on why that reaction hurts our classroom community. Gently and clearly I tried to convey my concern at what had just happened. I am an advocate for all the children in my room, not just the ones with self-control and winning personalities. I will defend the kid who can never find his pencil, who hasn't a clue how to organize his workspace, and whose social skills rank right up there with Atilla the Hun. How I treat the most challenging child is a measure of who I am as a teacher, as a person.

As an advocate for the children, I work to keep their perspective in mind. Bob Strachota wrote about this important philosophy in his book, *On Their Side: Helping Children Take Charge of Their Learning* (1996). His stance, "We're in this together. Let's work to find a solution to this problem" (91) made a profound difference in the way his class functioned together. He writes about blame and shows how it is counterproductive in the classroom. One difficult student, Josh, lost many privileges and spent time in the principal's office until Bob realized that "The only lesson they taught Josh was that he was failing again; plus they got in the way of our creating any bond that we could build on. . . . In their place I substituted more nurturance—and also more talk" (91). This empathetic perspective is not always easy, but the rewards are apparent in the willingness of children to work and excel.

After reading *On Their Side,* I had new strategies when I felt myself in an adversarial role with my class. The noise level during writing workshop was too high or the squirming during share had reached gale wind proportions. My first instinct was to resort to the old power play—"I want everyone sitting still and quiet!" But instead I viewed the problem from the perspective of a group member, not the group controller. "Donald is trying to share and not many of us are listening with respect," I said. "What can we do to help ourselves refocus?"

If time does not allow for a two-minute discussion, I may stop the group and do a fast energy restorer, such as the class clap or seat aerobics, for one minute. Fun and focus is the goal, not a punishment because they have failed as good listeners. It's not me in the big white hat trying to control a bunch of fidgety black hats. On Friday afternoons, I have to dig deep not to flash my sheriff's badge, but when control and authoritarian rule is the motivating force in the classroom everyone suffers, especially the exhausted teacher who feels like she is in this alone.

WE'RE IN THIS TOGETHER

Sometimes as teachers we see ourselves as distinct from the class. If it's a difficult group, in our frustration we tend to forget that it's difficult for everyone in the room, not just the experienced and taller one who is in charge. This thought was reinforced for me when I recently ran into an old friend as I boarded a plane. Passing down the aisle to my seat, I told her, "Have a safe and smooth flight." We laughed at my gratuitous comment and she wished me the same.

I shoved my coat into the overhead compartment and my classroom flashed through my mind. Each new school year is like boarding for a long flight. You're there for the duration. If the flight is bumpy and rough, everyone on board copes with the same turbulence. The crew or first-class passengers do not have a smoother ride—the plane jostles everyone. Likewise, when the skies are blue and the flight tranquil, all on board can appreciate the sense of security. The passengers on the classroom journey share the environment and receive its blessings and bumps. To ensure safe passage we must pay attention to the defining relationships. Their strength allows the class to withstand the storms and enjoy the times when the skies are clear.

When the teacher has a transformational relationship with each child based on mutual respect and understanding, classroom life prospers. This doesn't happen overnight. It starts before school begins and continues one smile at a time.

HOW CAN I HELP?

A year ago a dear friend had a heart attack while playing tennis with my husband. As part of his recuperation process, he attended cardio-care classes to help him learn to reduce the stress in his life. One of the strategies the doctors suggested for lowering stress was using four simple words: *How can I help?* It's amazing how these words send a different message to the brain, one that relieves tension and invites a sense of well-being. Of course, they can't be muttered through clenched teeth with a tone of sarcasm. When our question to our students is sincere—*How can I help?*—our bodies sense that we are in control and we relax. Offering support is a proactive stance that affects both the recipient and the giver. When I'm clear about my role—to help young learners—the job feels less stressful.

BEING NICE IS GOOD FOR YOUR HEALTH

Another health benefit of kindness was described in the newsletter *Focus on Health,* published by Blue Cross Blue Shield of Connecticut (1997). "According to a recent Harvard Medical School report, *being nice* can improve your health, reduce stress, and even help you live longer. . . . People who routinely help others have fewer trips to the doctor, according to a study conducted by the University of Massachusetts" (1). The articles went on to say that "Studies have shown that being nice actually increases the number of 1 lymphocytes that offset the effects of stress and make it possible for you to ward off simple infections and viruses. Physicians also report an increase in endorphins, mood-elevating chemicals produced by the body" (1).

Who would have guessed that being a kind and caring teacher is actually self-serving? So why not be nice? After years of experience, I know the days that are the most tiring and stressful are the days when I run out of *nice.* I've learned to be more aware of the signals—a light flashes on like when my car is low on gas—and I find ways to have the class help me replenish my *nice* supply.

FOCUS ON THE KIDS DOING IT RIGHT

One way I've found to restock my supply of nice is to focus on the kids who are doing it right. For example, as I attempt to explain the final directions before work begins, I feel like I am shouting into a heavy headwind. I stop, take a deep breath, and raise my hand. The class knows this signal: "Stop, look, listen, and smile." Eventually, even Marissa stops chatting and looks at me. "I need your help," I say with absolute truth. "I am running out of nice and I need your help to get it back. I feel like I am being ignored and I am only noticing the kids who are talking or fidgeting. If you are sitting quietly and listening to directions, I need to notice you. Please raise your hand and help me focus on who is doing it right." Many hands go up, even ones that should not be in the air. But there is a renewed commitment to get back on course. And

I know I have to be brief and get them started on their projects. At least my reservoir of nice has been momentarily restored.

FOCUS ON WHAT EACH CHILD CAN DO

About once or twice a year I find myself not only out of nice, but even worse—in the deficit mode. I look at my class and see them as half empty vessels. I only notice what they can't do and find little pleasure in their measly accomplishments. I can't always know what pushed me into this negative frame of mind, but I hate it. When I feel like I'm in the wrong profession and start to wonder what to do when I grow up, I know it's time to do some real work on my thinking. Seeing the children through mud-colored glasses doesn't serve them any better than it serves me. This year when the deficit virus hit, I was able to laugh about it with a colleague who had also been infected. We clearly knew who had the problem . . . we did! Our classes had not changed in any dramatic way—our view of them had. And this time I could sense what had happened. I felt disconnected. Donning the mantle of a perfectionist, I had become a critical outsider—a sure way to defeat myself as a teacher. I needed to reconnect to each child.

Getting out of my own head and listening to my students with determined commitment swung my thinking the one hundred and eighty degrees it needed. I could chuckle again when Paul couldn't find his pencil or Cody tipped over the bin of folders. These things happen in a crowded space full of energetic young bodies. It didn't mean I was a worthless teacher or that learning had left with my laughter. I now noticed that this was only the second pencil Paul had lost that day and that Cody had begun the assignment without a reminder. The whole class seemed more productive and independent.

That nagging sense that all is *not* well may be a sign that changes are necessary. But whatever the problem, turning up my sonar can be the first step in finding the solution. Careful listening and focusing on what kids *can* do braids the rope into a stronger cord. In *Emotional Intelligence,* Daniel Goleman describes it this way:

> The synchrony between teachers and students indicates how much rapport they feel; studies in classrooms show that the closer the movement coordination between teacher and student, the more they felt friendly, happy, enthused, interested, and easygoing while interacting. In general, a high level of synchrony in an interaction means the people involved like each other. (116)

When I felt reconnected to the children and found pleasure in their company, I suddenly noticed each accomplishment, no matter how small.

WATCH YOUR LANGUAGE

I love the subtlety of the English language and the way a small accomplishment can be diminished when I change the word *small* to *measly*. This happens to children when we change the language we use to talk about and with them. Too often we rush to label children, and our pejorative words determine how we relate to them. I am learning to reframe how I talk about the children in my class and to use positive instead of negative words. For example, one year I had an overabundance of kids who preferred to be chiefs and very few willing to take orders. I found myself describing them as *bossy*, an irritating trait. Then one morning I realized that the children I considered bossy were the ones who were trying to be leaders. Thinking about a classroom of *potential leaders* seemed much more palatable than a classroom full of *bossy children*.

Closer observations of the children allow me to see past commonplace labels, such as *lazy*, to more accurate terms such as *disinterested* or *anxious*. The question then becomes Why? And how can I help? The disorganized child is often too involved to be bothered with details. His energy goes into more exciting activities, such as learning. The child who calls out and interrupts may be the enthusiastic extrovert who needs to process information by saying it. The *nosey* child is curious about the world. The better I know each child, the better my chances of giving him strategies to help solve behavior issues.

Say What You Mean and Mean What You Say

The language we use *with* children must also be thoughtful. Chapter 9 of Ruth Charney's *Teaching Children to Care* (1992) is called "Empowering Language: Say What You Mean & Mean What You Say." She uses examples from the classroom to demonstrate the importance of supporting our words with actions. She recommends six

guidelines for using language to affirm meaning and action:

Keep demands simple—keep them short.
Say what you mean—make your demands appropriate.
Mean what you say—dignify your words with actions.
Remind only twice—the third time 'you're out.'
Speak directly—tell children 'nonnegotiables,' don't ask.
Use words that invite cooperation. (151)

Children need clear expectations and teacher follow-through on what she says. Otherwise, our words are dandelion puffs in the breeze.

I try to say what I mean and mean what I say, and I also try very hard not to be *mean* when I say it. Even at the end of a long, exasperating day, mean is out.

Use an Artful Critique

The way we talk with children each day shapes their sense of who they are. Our words are mirrors reflecting back to them how they are viewed by one of the most powerful and influential adults in their lives. Our words can kindle or crush, empower or embarrass. Daniel Goleman offers sage advice for critiquing that respects the importance of the relationship. He writes that "an artful critique focuses on what a person has done and can do rather than reading a mark of character into a job poorly done" (1995, 153). He quotes Harry Levinson, a psychoanalyst turned corporate consultant, whose advice for giving an artful critique follows:

Be specific.
Offer a solution.
Be present.
Be sensitive.

Global comments about behavior are damaging to developing egos. A child may be having a problem *today*, but certainly doesn't need a history lesson ("This is your tenth paper without a name" or "Why can't you remember to hang up your jacket?"). A helpful, problem solving approach supports learners and makes enduring relationships possible.

DEVELOPMENTAL CONSIDERATIONS

Developmental considerations are another key to understanding and enjoying children. When I know that six-year-olds fall off their chairs, I am much more accepting when Cybil topples onto the floor again. When I started teaching second grade, I wondered why so many kids erased holes in their papers. What was wrong with them? Then I read about their need for perfection. Erasing is typical and expected behavior. Why do third graders have so much energy and move around the room so fast? Can't they walk like adults? Answer: No. Children have specific developmental phases and we might just as well know what they are and embrace them—otherwise we are doing a major disservice to the children and ourselves. It's exhausting to be out of sync with developmental demands. Can you imagine spending your day trying to teach multiplication to a kindergarten class? Or asking fourth graders to sit in a circle on the floor and sing "The Farmer in the Dell"?

Every classroom teacher needs to know the developmental patterns for her grade level. The first book I read when I changed to second grade was *Your Seven Year Old,* by Louise Bates Ames and Carol Haber. This book is one in a series that covers each year of a child's life from birth through adolescence and offers excellent developmental information. *Yardsticks,* by Chip Wood (1994), is another practical resource. As a third-grade teacher, I made copies of the eight- and nine-year-old pages to share with parents. I wanted all of us to know what to expect from the children as they grow and mature through the school year.

Understanding developmental issues for children is critical to our expectations, but it is not as straightforward as it may sound. Jane Healy writes in *Endangered Minds* that at any one grade level there may be a four-year span in reading levels (1990, 298). When Heidi Hays Jacobs, a professor at Columbia University, talked to our staff she told us that at the primary level there can be an emotional age range from two to twenty. I could immediately think of one child in my room who would fit well into a preschool setting at times and another who could probably handle living on her own in a studio apartment. Developmental levels give us the edges of the jigsaw puzzle and guide us as we fill in the picture of each child.

One year in my second grade I had three boys who were several months younger than most of the class. Academically they were fine, but their immaturity quietly surfaced each morning as I read a picture book aloud to the class. Jack, Robert, and Mark usually sat at the back of the group. They listened attentively, but I began to notice that they never were in the same place by the end of the story as they were when we had started. Without even realizing it, all three shifted around at the back of the group as I read. The rest of the class was riveted on the illustrations in the books, so were unaware of the silent shuffling. I was thankful for the developmental books I had read about children at this age. I knew it was much more difficult for students to sit still than it was for them to run and jump. Jack, Robert, and Mark were not misbehaving as they slowly and silently scooted around the back of the group. Their movement was necessary for them to listen carefully. In order to stay focused, they needed to move.

Our expectations must be based on the developmental level of the children. Every once in a while, just before a much-needed vacation or when my reserves of laughter are running low, I'll watch the energetic, bouncy kids come down the hall, totally absorbed in loud and animated conversations about movies, sports, or delicious gossip. "They're acting like children!" I'll think in dismay. Ninety-nine times out of a hundred my inane thought makes me chuckle. Then I am ready again to be their patient teacher who trusts that peace and order will be shortly restored. This is just a noisy and needed transition before the next burst of concentration.

TEACHERS SHAPE THE WAY CHILDREN VIEW THEMSELVES. WHEN I looked into Mrs. Finkbinder's eyes as an unsure seven-year-old, I believed in myself because she believed in me. She saw a pretty little girl who loved school and knew how to be a fine student. She looked past my crooked teeth and home permanent. What she saw in me was what I wanted to become.

Children need to feel connected to their teacher in ways that empower them and enrich their lives. There is no bell curve for self-esteem and loving to learn, nor should we impose an artificial scarcity on our affection because it has not been earned. Children who spend their days in our company need to feel understood, appreciated, and valued. The next chapter describes ways to get to know the children in our class ASAP. The sooner a resilient relationship can be established, the sooner the classroom bike can soar like the ones in *E.T.*—high above the school, over the trees, and beyond.

3

Getting to Know Each Child

R ecently the gym teacher and I were talking about the children in my class. Kelly has them twice a week for thirty-five minutes and sees a different child in that setting than the one I see in the classroom.

"You know who strikes me as spoiled and used to getting his own way?" she asked. I was curious to hear. "Patrick," she said.

I did not expect her to say Patrick. He is the youngest in the class and in his family of three children. Developmentally, he is immature and small of stature, but academically he is a solid student and usually cheerful and co-operative. I've never thought about him as spoiled. As I talked with Kelly about Patrick and shared the details of his life, she began to see him in a new light.

To build a strong relationship with children, we must know their stories. The narrative of their lives brings them to life and makes them unique. We need to know that Desiree can climb a rope all the way to the top of the gym or that Tim lives with his grandparents. All the bits and pieces of their young lives fit together to create the children who greet us each day.

This chapter is about getting to know those children as quickly and thoroughly as possible. Learning about each child is not a simple, one-step process, but more like a yearlong research project. It needs to be our priority as we take off through the starting gate each fall. Understanding each child is the keystone for a resilient and transformational relationship. The bed-rock for that understanding is to know as much as we can about the child and how he learns. This chapter offers suggestions to help you get to know your kids as soon as possible so that your appreciation and affection for them can bloom.

BEFORE SCHOOL STARTS

I begin the "getting to know you" process before the school year starts. I like to have an initial sense of each child before I begin our relationship in person. This doesn't mean that I will believe all the positive *or* negative things I hear about a child. I know there may be an unrevealed picture behind the more obvious one, and I want to be alert to all possibilities.

Talking with Previous Teachers

Teachers can give important insights. For the past two years, our teachers have met in August for an articulation day. As a third-grade teacher, I meet with the six second-grade teachers one at a time to get a quick synopsis of each incoming child. After that, I meet with fourth-grade teachers to talk about the children going to them. We often wonder how we ever started the year without taking this time to talk about children. Our conversations run the gamut from the child as a learner to social issues, health problems, and parental concerns. I take notes during these conferences—one child on each page of my journal. This journal becomes one of my most important resources during the year.

Reading Through School Records

Next, I sit with the files in the office and browse through the records. I jot down the names of the parents and siblings. It helps me understand Joseph better if I know he is the middle child with an older and younger sister. It's important to me to know that Chris is an only child or that Monica has a sister who is sixteen years older than she is. I like to know that Justin's parents speak Russian at home and that Erik came from Norway when he was in kindergarten. To give me a flavor of home life, I like to learn which parents work out of the house and the kinds of jobs they do. I also want to know the birth dates of the children, to have a better picture where they might be on the developmental continuum. All these factors affect their lives, and the more I know, the more I can appreciate who they are. As I fill the pages in my journal, the story of each child begins to unfold.

Postcards to the Students

Healthy relationships are reciprocal, so I want the students to get a sense of who I am. About a week before school starts I send them postcards. For young children, mail is a rare treat, so the time I take writing to them is well spent. Here is a sample of a postcard message:

Hi Max,

Welcome to third grade!
I hope you've had a fun summer. I did.
Next Tuesday, please bring a healthy snack,
a favorite book, and a photo or drawing from your summer.
I have many interesting activities planned as we get to know each other.
I look forward to meeting you next week.

Some of my colleagues send longer, more detailed letters. Whatever we send, that first greeting assures children that we are committed to making the year ahead a good one and gives them a glimpse of who we are.

Meeting Children for a Brief Hello

The day before school begins, we schedule an hour when parents bring their children to school to meet the teacher and visit the classroom. Observing the interaction between the parent and the child gives me more information about each new student. When Liza's three-year-old brother climbed up on a desk to try to open the gerbil cage, I had a fleeting idea what life might be like for Liza at home with two active younger brothers. Carl pulled on his mother's skirt and whispered to her not to tell me that he was shy about starting in a new school. When Jill wrote her name on the large chart paper with a backward J, her mother squirmed and said, "She knows which way it should go." She took the marker out of Jill's hand and quickly made the correction. Jill looked at the floor.

Each brief encounter adds to my storehouse of information. My early ideas may be wrong, but in many cases, as the year evolves, my hunches prove valid. All the other factors in their lives have an impact on our relationship. The melodious and harmonious duet I hope to play with each of them during the year depends on what instrument and musical background they bring to school each day. Whether I choose to play a harp to their flute or a flute to their bassoon, my decisions require as much information as I can gather.

THE FIRST WEEK OF SCHOOL

Parent Questions

My first letter home to parents the week school begins asks them to help me get to know their child better by answering these three questions:

- What are your goals for your child this year?
- What does your child do in his/her free time?
- What would you like me to know about your child?

I've asked parents to answer these questions for the past nine years and I'm always impressed and sometimes even moved by their responses. Some parents are remarkably in tune with their child and their description meshes easily with the child I'm getting to know:

> Walker is sometimes quiet which means he is thinking intensely. You need to talk to him and he will open up completely. Treat him in an adult manner and he'll give all he can in school to his peers and to you!

Sometimes the parent responses clue me in to issues that are causing problems at home:

> Alicia seems to think she is no longer a "little" girl. She doesn't want to look "cute," but cool. I am having a hard time dealing with this, especially since she is only 8 and not 13 or 14!

Last year, Emily's mom wrote at length about her child's giftedness. I took a mental double take. In the first two weeks of school Emily had shown no signs of giftedness unless it was in her flair for the dramatic and her uncanny ability to seek attention in inappropriate ways. Where was this creative child her mother described? I love mysteries and I was determined to uncover this disguised genius. Low and behold, within a few weeks of watching and nurturing signs of intelligent life, I began to see what her mother meant. Little sparks of creativity and insight appeared at random moments. Emily noticed details in stories everyone else overlooked and offered original and thoughtful ideas to reference charts. She began to show a side of herself I could have missed if I hadn't been alerted by her mom. It's easy to dismiss parent stories of talent and unique gifts as just another parent blinded by love. But I find there is often a kernel of truth in what parents tell me and I welcome their version of the child. The school setting has a way of masking the gifts of some children. With parent insights and a little extra scrutiny on my part, I can glimpse the picture hidden beneath the more obvious one.

This fall, a student new to our school befuddled me with his behaviors. He buzzed around the room like a mosquito looking for a place to land. Thank heavens for the letter his mother wrote to me the end of the first week.

> My son Philip has moved many times with us. He changed school four times by now. I hope he is adjusting well. At home I don't see problems. He tells me everything is wonderful. But sometimes, he is very protective of me and does not want me to worry. Please, if you notice that he is not making friends or prefers to be alone, let me know. He will not be the first one to approach. Philip is a kind, loving boy. He has a *heart of gold*.

I found it easier to be patient and supportive of Philip as I heard his mother's words in my head. Again, here was a child who was doing the best he could.

The majority of parents are eager to write about their child and many have ended their letters with "Thank you for asking."

Observing and Eavesdropping

The first week of school is intense. To get the year off to a solid start, there are so many things we must tell the children. The paradox is that this is a time when teachers need to do their most careful listening. The challenge is to structure the day so there are opportunities to get to know the children in the context of meaningful activities. One way is to involve kids in activities that allow for interaction and require minimum supervision once they get started. As I move about the room monitoring who needs help, mopping up spills, and offering suggestions, I am able to collect crucial data about the children. I once heard a psychologist friend describe her work as "an all day listener." My mind leaped on the phrase. "Aha!" I thought. "That's why I am so tired at the end of the day! I am an all day listener!" And listening takes a lot of stamina. The first week of school I try to soak up their words like a daffodil in the April sun. Their words will help me get to know them better.

Surveys and graphs are an easy but fruitful activity. Few provisions are needed—a class list for each child, construction paper, and glue—and the activity can be adapted to any grade level. Kids enjoy the freedom of walking around the room and asking each other their questions. Several questions from this year were "Have you ever been on an airplane?" "Have you ever gone off the high dive at a swimming pool?" and "Which do you like better, pizza or tacos?"

As children tally and graph their survey results, I observe their ability to follow directions, organize their work, and extend an activity with their own ideas. Which children are unable to think of a survey question? Which children are unable to organize the survey results without support? Who moves through the assignment as sleekly as a seal down a water slide?

While the children work on their surveys and graphs over several days, I have an opportunity to chat informally and eavesdrop—a necessary skill for teachers. When children engage in natural, uninhibited conversation there is much to learn. A quick note in my journal helps me remember the amazing tidbits I overhear.

Having children draw or paint self-portraits is another productive first week activity. Teachers can learn so much as they observe students working and talking together. When the colorful and detailed portraits are hung around the room, it begins to look more like home.

Interviews

In addition to the informal listening that I do all day, during the first week of school I schedule a time to interview each child while the rest of the class is reading silently or engaged in another independent reading activity. This one-on-one time may be difficult to find, but it accelerates the "getting to know you" process. I get an opportunity to listen deeply to a child and the child has an opportunity to get to know me better. A reading interview provides valuable and necessary information and guides instructional planning. Here are some of the questions I have used at different times. Keep in mind that fewer questions may yield more information than many.

READING INTERVIEW QUESTIONS
How did you learn to read?
When was a time when reading was fun for you?
When was a time when reading was hard for you?
Who is your reading partner at home?
Where do you usually read at home?
Where are the books in your house?
What do you think you do well as a reader?
Who do you know who is a really good reader? Why?
What would you like to do better?

It is the meaning that I make from the interview that matters. What have I learned about the child as a reader? How will I help this child make a lasting connection to literacy?

LEARNING ABOUT CHILDREN THROUGH CLASS SHARES

As ideal as it is to sit with each child individually, most of the time our plans must include small groups or the entire class. A convenient way to acquire new information about each child is through class shares. I want to establish the expectations and procedures for whole class shares the very first day, as they are an integral part of our learning community. Unless the children can sit quietly and listen thoughtfully to each other, our time together would be like a room without windows. Thriving relationships rely on a flow of information moving back and forth among the participants. Whole class conversations provide the forum for discussing meaningful information. There are three kinds of whole class shares that help me know each child better and build our classroom community: morning meeting, end of the day share, and curriculum shares.

Morning Meeting

Our morning ritual is to sit in a circle and greet each other by name. Based on the model I learned in workshops with Chip Wood from the Northeast Foundation for Children,* our morning circle welcomes each child and provides a transition back into school life. The "person of the day" in my class chooses the greeting from about a dozen favorite possibilities. She greets the person next to her, for example, with a high five and a "Good morning, Jared!" Jared then turns to the child on his left and passes the greeting along with the high five. In this ritual, every child hears his or her name as the day begins.

My third-grade class likes to do a clapping rhythm while they chant a good morning greeting for each child around the circle. They especially enjoy when the greeting starts with one child, and as each name is added around the circle that child joins in the clapping. The voices gain in volume like a band in a parade coming down the street. This morning ritual signals the start of a new day.

Following the pattern of the Northeast Foundation morning meeting, four children in the class can sign up for a short share each morning before we begin. They tell one sentence of their news and then call on children who ask questions. This allows the children to find out the information that interests them and they listen better to each other than when one children rattles on with details and protracted descriptions. Here's a sample from a recent share:

> BRANDON: I'm going to Chicago. (*He calls on Margaret.*)
>
> MARGARET: Why are you going to Chicago?
>
> BRANDON: I'm going to visit my grandparents. (*Calls on John.*)
>
> JOHN: Is it a special occasion?
>
> BRANDON: It's their wedding anniversary. (*Calls on Jane.*)

* The Northeast Foundation for Children (71 Montague Rd., Greenfield, MA; www .responsiveclassroom.org) publish a newsletter, *Responsive Classroom,* and a number of fine books about establishing a solid social curriculum.

JANE: How will you get there? Will you go on a plane?
BRANDON: Yes, we're leaving after school today.

These brief interchanges let the children focus on what they're curious to know and give me a chance to notice their social and language skills. Their questions are often more thoughtful and to the point than the ones in my head.

On Monday and Friday mornings, rather than four children sharing with the above format, we do a whole class whip around the circle after the greeting. On Monday mornings children are invited to tell something about their weekend. On Friday they may share something they are looking forward to in the coming weekend. I like learning about their lives out of school and I know they enjoy hearing what their classmates are doing. Children may pass without pressure to share. I take my turn and tell something about my life out of school life. With the time restraints of the day, each student is limited to not much more than a sound bite, but even that keeps our communication channels open. During or after the share I may jot down student comments in my journal that I don't want to forget.

End of the Day Share

Dismissal has never been a time of day I felt I handled with style. I tried a number of strategies over the years and nothing seemed to quell the frantic feeling as children did all those last minute things before scurrying for the bus. My friend next door, Anne Nesbitt, explained to me how her class ended each day with a share. It sounded so simple. It is.

I need to back up one step and tell you how boring and trite I find the typical elementary school show-and-tell. I always felt guilty if I did it with the class because I knew I wasn't being a good listener, nor were the children. Unless I acted like James Marshall's Viola Swamp, they didn't pay attention to each other. However, I knew kids loved to drag in special things from home to share. Anne's low-key and simple solution transformed the tempo of the end of the day from heavy metal to New Age.

Children sit in the circle on the floor after they have organized what they need to go home. Anyone who wants to may share. The person of the day keeps track of the order children come to the circle and is responsible for calling on who goes next. Children may share something they've brought from home, something they did in school, such as a picture they're drawn, or do a talking share. Some days half the class wants to share. Other days it may be as few as five children. Earlier in the afternoon I ask who wants to share so I can reserve enough time. Again, each share is rather brief, but kids seem satisfied if they get a chance to show what they brought in and explain something about it. The spotlight is so important to some children I think they would share lint off the floor and embellish it with a little story. This tells me that they really need this attention and sense of belonging. The class is happy to relax and learn more about each other at the end of the day. The expectations and procedures are clear and they can count on a time when kids and their ideas are the content.

Curriculum Shares

When I returned to classroom teaching from a townwide position in 1990, I complained to my friend Anne, my advisor on dismissal, that the children were not putting enough effort and pride into their reading response sheets. Their work seemed too rote and routine.

"Do they have a chance to share them?" Anne asked. "If you want them to care about their work, they need to show others what they have accomplished."

Bingo! Anne had hit the nail on the head. Work that goes into a folder or maybe home to the kitchen refrigerator doesn't require the same effort and precision as work talked about with peers. In the past I had often asked kids to share artwork or other projects, but I had failed to understand the value of time spent talking about daily assignments.

So our reading time ended with a period when children could share their reading response sheets, tell about a picture they had drawn, and/or read what they had written about the book. A new energy appeared as the children labored over their response sheets. As pride and pleasure developed, so did a class assessment list for "What Makes a Good Response Sheet." Together we set standards for their work, elevating and clarifying expectations. I referred to their standards frequently before they set to work. Sharing work in a re spectful circle of peers nudges routine requirements to a deeper level of commitment. Like a high tide raises all boats, group enthusiasm and support raises the level of effort and desire to achieve.

During the course of a week, we may meet in a circle to share drawings from observation journals, letters home, facts from research, book recommendations, and other writing from math or science journals. If I want to send the message that something in particular is important, we meet and talk about it or share it in the group. This process helps to build a strong classroom community, and it also gives me insights and information about individual children. Once the ground rules for group behavior are set as nonnegotiable, I can put my energy into careful listening as children speak. I want to know what they are thinking. Whether I am listening to their words one-on-one or in a group, my appreciation and understanding of them grows.

REFERENCE CHARTS

Children need to feel comfortable and confident as learners to maximize their learning curve. The better they know their teacher, their peers, the routines, and the expectations, the better they are able to put their energy into learning and growing. I want my relationship with each child to allow for smoothly flowing energy back and forth between us. To help give them a clear under-standing of the routines and expectations, we construct a number of reference charts together. One of the first reference charts developed by my class is called "Ways We Want Our Class to Be." The first few days of school we define how we hope to work and learn together for the school year. Reference charts for "What Makes a Good Journal Entry" or "Rubrics for Letters Home" give the students a solid sense of what is required. The rules and expectations are explicit, defined by them and for them. Some reference charts hang on the wall to serve as reminders, such as:

What to Do When You're Stuck in Writing
Morning Responsibilities
Kinds of Stories
High-Frequency Words
Steps for Research Projects
What We Can Write About Books
What Makes a Good Book

Others are more of a celebration and mark our history as a learning commu-nity, such as

Read Alouds We Have Enjoyed
Authors We Have Studied
What We Know About Roald Dahl
What We've Learned About Bats
Beautiful Language from Books
Our Favorite Idioms
How We've Changed as Readers

The charts hang in the room as long as they are useful and decorate the walls with evidence of growth and change.

LEARNING ABOUT CHILDREN
THROUGH THEIR WRITING

Often our busy classroom lives squeeze out time to really listen to each child. Having them write their thoughts is the next best thing and sometimes uncovers a level of thinking that is even more honest and authentic.

Letter Journal

I began using a letter journal with my class several years ago. It is simply a spiral notebook where the children write periodic letters to me on a variety of topics and I respond. The children I inherit from the previous grade have usually written a journal entry each morning as they started their day. A daily journal entry for another school year seemed more than they could bear. Since the students do a lot of writing in curriculum journals, I needed another place for them to write about other classroom issues.

For example, one Tuesday morning the children arrived upset and impatient to tell me how horrendous the substitute teacher had been the day before. I knew the sub by her reputation and would have preferred someone else, but many teachers were out for grade-level meetings and I had no choice. I knew the children needed an opportunity to air their grievances, yet I didn't want to start the morning as the "complaint department." Instead, I passed out their letter journals and asked them to please tell me about what had made Monday so hard for them with the substitute, Mrs. Swamp. "If I had time, I would interview each one of you and hear what made yesterday feel so awful. Since we don't have that time, please jot down your thinking for me and I'll write back to you."

Samantha wrote:

> Mrs. Swamp is the worst substitute I've ever had. I rate myself a 4. And I rate her a *zero*. I won once in bingo. Mrs. Swamp never talks. She always yells and doesn't let me laugh.

A minute or two after I asked the children to write, Dan popped up and put his journal in the finished work basket. Since he is usually a quiet and thoughtful child, I asked him if he was sure he had been able to say what he wanted to in such a short time. He nodded and returned to his seat. Later when I opened his journal I found this entry:

> Dear Mrs. Skolnick,
> I hated it. I missed you. Dan

He had said it all. I was relieved that I had not asked him to add more. And if I hadn't asked the children to write to me, I wouldn't have know how Dan felt.

Letter journals are a place for children to share what's on their mind. If they want to write to me about something, they put their journal in the basket on the corner of my desk and I get back to them. This is a way for them to let me know something that they could not talk about in front of the other children. Several times a year I'll ask kids to finish a line: "The best thing about our class is . . ." or "The worst thing about out class is . . ." Although I dislike posing questions that ask for negative replies, I have found their responses worthwhile.

Several years ago at a workshop a teacher complained about the entries her students made in their journals. "Their best entry is the one they write the first day of school when I ask them what they are looking forward to in second grade. After that, they don't seem to care as much about what they write."

I think I know why. When the children wrote to their teacher the first day of school, they believed she would read their letters and take their responses seriously. In time, they realized that what they wrote was just a writing exercise and didn't affect what happened in the classroom. Of course, their answers became perfunctory.

That conversation left a mark on my thinking. I want to ensure that children in my class know what they write in their letter journal is important and that I listen just as carefully to what they write as I listen to what they say.

Weekend News

Writing about their weekend is another way we can get to know our students better. As the children read their entries to the class, I am able to learn about their interests out of school, how their family spends time together, as well as learn about how they are growing and changing as a writer. When I moved to a higher grade level and stopped scheduling time for weekend news, I built a time to talk and share into our Monday morning. Events over the weekend can sometimes influence the behavior of children into the weekdays. I began to notice a pattern in Julie's behavior whenever her adult sister visited on the weekend. Sleepovers and birthday parties can also leave telltale signs on Monday behaviors. Writing or talking about the weekend knits the classroom community back together after the two-day separation and gives another glimpse into the lives of the children.

Letters Home

After several years of talking to colleagues about the letters their students wrote home each week, I finally tried it with my class. I recommend to you letters home with the hope that your class is already doing them. If not, it won't take you long to initiate them. Again, the activity is simple but the rewards are great. On Friday, the class and I brainstorm the week's events. Then the children write a letter to their parents telling them about activities that they thought were important. The letters home journal is a three-pronged notebook with notebook paper. If the journal is not returned by the following Friday, they can write on notebook paper and add the letter to their journal later.

I request that parents write back to the children before the journal is returned to school. In an attempt to protect kids from overzealous parents who tend to leap at every surface error, the students staple this typed letter in the front of the journal:

Dear Mom and Dad,

Please read my letter about the week at school. Remember that it is a rough draft. I tried to print neatly so it is easy for you to read. When I finished writing, I reread my letter to check for

capital letters at the beginning of sentences

capital letters for names, dates, and places

proper punctuation at the end of sentences

proper spelling for words we have studied

Does it make sense?

I hope you will help me notice progress that I am making as a writer and not be too critical of my mistakes.

Please write a brief note back to me. Mrs. Skolnick says she will not edit your letter. She has trained herself to read through mistakes and appreciate the message.

Also, please help me remember to return this letter journal to school by next Friday so I can add a new letter.

Thank you.

Hopefully this note helps parents understand that this is basically first draft writing by a developing writer. The other option would be to have children recopy their letters after they have been edited. Time is too valuable and the letters would get shorter each week. Years ago when recopying was fashionable, I soon realized that it inhibited young writers and many errors remained unchanged. I do read through each letter quickly and require students to fix missed punctuation or misspelled high-frequency words. Otherwise, the letters are spontaneous and authentic, if imperfect.

After about a month of writing letters, the class and I developed a rubric for what makes a high-quality letter. I wanted the standards to be explicit, and when children brought their letters to me or their peers for a quick edit, I didn't want to say the same things every week. Of course, I still do, but at least my words are supported by the reference chart on the wall. We talked together about what a basic letter home would be as I wrote their ideas on chart paper. They agreed that the lowest score would be just a list (see number one below). As the rating of the rubric went higher, so did the demands for the writer. The chart is slightly different each year, but here is the one my present class developed:

RUBRICS FOR LETTERS HOME

4   Extended sentences
    Tell more specific details (who, what, where, when, how, and why)
    Words spelled correctly
    Proper punctuation
    Really exciting

3   Spelling mostly correct
    Punctuation mostly correct
    Tell why we did a project or activity

2   Spelling improves a little
    A short opinion is included
    Printing improves—better spacing

1   Five sentences
    A list of events
    Dull and boring
    Not best printing
    Spelling not good

This is our first rubric for letters home. An older grade level may create a more demanding one. Later in the year we will revisit this rubric and see if our standards have changed. This initial chart gives us a common language and goals for the letters. I refer to the rubric before the class begins writing. It is a reminder of the standard and they use it for self-assessment.

To help raise the bar on letter quality, on some Fridays I write to my own family using a transparency. The class and I critique my letter and offer suggestions for making it more of a 4. Sometimes I will ask three or four volunteers to read their letters aloud. Children often get fresh ideas for how to improve their letters as they listen to the letters of their classmates. A few children usually move out in front of the class on the developmental writing continuum and light the way for the rest. For example, when Lital included her opinion of the new read aloud book, the children decided that giving an opinion made the letter more interesting. When our pet hamster, Ralph S. Hamster, escaped, Alexandra described the frantic search under the cubbies, in the corners, and behind the bookcase. Her letter highlighted how specific details make an event sound more exciting. She exploded the moment even before we had talked about that as a writing strategy. When the children wrote about Ralph's unplanned escape and miraculous rescue, their letters home reached a new level of concentration.

Most parents write letters back each week. These letters also give me new information about the child and what's going on at home. I appreciate the time the parents take with their letters and know that the children do, as well. For children whose parents are too busy to jot a note back, I ask them to request a special hug instead.

Surveys

When time feels precious and there is general information from each child that I need, a survey serves my purpose. Below is a survey I used to learn more about each child as a reader at the beginning of the school year.

READING SURVEY QUESTIONS

1. I like to choose my own books to read.
   Always   Sometimes   Never

2. I can usually find good books to read.
   Yes   No

3. I like to read chapter books.
   Yes   Not yet

4. I can read silently for about _____ minutes.

5. I read at home
   Every day   Every few days   Not if I can help it

6. At home I like to read
   In bed   On the floor   In a comfortable chair

7. The kinds of books I like to read include
   _____ Chapter books   _____ Nonfiction
   _____ Books with pictures   _____ Animal stories
   _____ Jokes and riddle books _____ Mysteries
   _____ Sports books   _____ Humorous
   other _____

8. Books and authors I have read:
   _____ Cam Jansen   _____ Goosebumps
   _____ Horrible Harry   _____ Wayside School
   _____ Patricia Reilly Giff   _____ Baby-sitters Club
   other _____

Another survey sheet that I ask kids to fill out several times during the year gives me a different type of information:

HOW I SEE MYSELF

1. I follow rules even without a teacher around.
   Always   Sometimes   Not yet

2. I get to work without reminders.
   Always   Sometimes   Not yet

3. I walk in the hall even without a teacher around.
   Always   Sometimes   Not yet

4. I follow directions without reminders.
   Always   Sometimes   Not yet

5. I think I am a successful student.
   Always   Sometimes   Not yet

6. Other kids know I am a responsible student.
   Always   Sometimes   Not yet

7. Something you should know about me is:

I first used this survey with a second-grade class about the third week of school. Danny was a new, quiet child from Colorado. I was so glad I had added the seventh question to the survey because Danny wrote: "I am a good student but nobody knows." My heart sank. I had an important job ahead to help him feel noticed and valued. In his new school setting, Danny needed a chance in the spotlight. I try to remember to ask an open-ended question at the end of a survey in case my questions don't uncover what's significant to the child.

RATING SCALES

From the first morning of school I begin to ask kids to assess themselves and to show their rating with their fingers. I might introduce this activity asking a few quick personal questions. This is how that introduction to finger rating might go:

> I would love the chance to talk with each of you about your summer. We will be sharing some things from your summer later, but I would like a quick idea right now. You are going to let me know by showing me with your fingers. Here's the question: How was your summer vacation? Give it a four if it was one of your best vacations ever. Give it a three if you enjoyed most of it and had a good time. Give it a two if it was only so-so. Rate it a one if it was dreadful. Ready? Please show me a four, three, two, or one. [I pause and survey the hands. If someone has failed to do the rating, I will ask them if they need me to remind them of the rating scale. I want everyone to feel I have seen their rating.] Here's my second question: How has the day gone for you so far? Please give it a four if you have felt comfortable and at home. Please rate it a three if you feel OK, but are still a little nervous. Please rate it a two if you are still a little worried about what I might ask you to do. Show me a one if you are still really uncomfortable and can only think about how many more minutes. [Again I pause and survey the finger ratings.]

I will probably ask three or four questions to be sure everyone understands how to do it and that I expect their participation. Some of the rating scales I use often are:

- Rate your effort as we worked during reading (or writing, and so on).
- Rate how well you cooperated with your partner.
- Rate how well you understand the assignment.
- Rate how you score the work you accomplished during reading.
- Rate how well you came to the morning meeting.
- Rate how you feel about getting started on the assignment.

Each time before I ask the kids to rate themselves, I give a quick definition of what each score means for that specific question. I try to add a bit of humor if I can. For example, after a lengthy explanation about how to do a reading project, I asked the children to rate how they were feeling about getting started on the project. Here was my scale:

Rate yourself a four if you are eager to get to work and you know just what to do.

Rate yourself a three if you think you know what to do but you're not absolutely positive.

Rate yourself a two if you are feeling uncertain about what to do and you think everyone else already knows.

Rate yourself a one if you wish I had never dreamed up this crazy assignment.

Children enjoy having a chance to rate their feelings and opinions. I like this kind of rating because it gives me a chance to see what everyone is thinking without taking the time to ask individually. If I'm surprised by the rating of some children, I seek them out later to find out why they voted as they did.

Rating with fingers is a quick way to give kids a sense of accountability and to check on their thinking. I use a similar rating scale when children complete written assignments. I like to have children pause to reflect on their effort, their process, and their final product and to write that number on the top of their paper. Sometimes we've created the rubric together and sometimes I invent it as I do with the finger rating. If I am in sync with the class, the rating scale will be similar to all the other ones we have done. In this way I find out who is being too hard on themselves and who is being too accepting. Asking children to self-evaluate gives me a fast look at how they view themselves as learners.

GETTING TO KNOW EACH CHILD IS A WORTHY VENTURE. ALONG the way, I am able to discover their strengths and specialties. Sometimes finding the stellar quality in a child is like trying to find the needle in the haystack. It takes tremendous effort and the light of the noonday sun before I see the shiny glint of silver among the confusion of hay. Other children present themselves as gifts. Their mere presence brightens the day. Our responsibility as a teacher is to enjoy and respect all learners. They all need and deserve our gentle care.

Tuesdays with Morrie, by Mitch Albom, captures the essence of the relationship between the teacher and the child: "Have you ever really had a teacher? One who saw you as a raw but precious thing, a jewel that, with wisdom, could be polished to a proud shine?" (1997, 192).

Getting to know the children from the inside out is part of the polishing process. Their relationship with us, based on honor and knowledge, allows all of us to shine.

4

The Relationships Between and Among the Students

*A*ugust is a month of high hopes. As I look forward to the new school year, I am confident that this year will be the best ever. I scan the list of names and imagine a group of cooperative and enthusiastic learners.

"Shall I tell you about some of your new class?" a well-meaning colleague offers.

"No thanks. Not yet," I reply. I like the class I've created in my mind. I'll stick with those imaginary kids for a few more days. Sometimes I think the ostrich has the right idea.

As a fresh young teacher many years ago, I knew the kind of class that would work best for me. I wanted the boys to act like girls and I wanted the girls to act like secretaries. Everyone would be content to stay seated, quiet, attentive, and busy. The agenda was mine and cooperative learning meant they cooperated with me.

I am happy and grateful to report that my ideal class has undergone an evolution. Just as I no longer wear miniskirts and a long bouncy ponytail, I no longer look for conformity and uniformity. I understand the toll that extracts from children. What works best for me has shifted to what works best for the class. And ultimately, that works best for me as well. We're on the same team.

A class in the key of C major, with no sharps or flats, now sounds boring. I want a class in D flat major. I want the richness and variability of playing with six flats, using all eighty-eight keys on the piano. The key of C with no sharps and flats is just that . . . flat. I want a room full of children eager to discover their strengths and special talents, and curious about their world, and curious about each other—not professional secretaries. I want big inquisitive question marks, not complacent periods.

43

Last week my third graders were working with their kindergarten writing partners. Earnest mentors to their young friends, they take their role seriously. Alexandra and Jenna huddled over Jenna's picture trying to figure out which words they wanted to use to tell about it. Max was helping Margot with her story. As the four children worked back in a corner I overhear Alexandra say to Max, "Just tell her the letter, Max. She's struggling." Max smiled at Alexandra and nodded. My heart struck a D flat major chord. In that moment, I was the luckiest teacher alive.

I was blessed to teach with an incredible teacher, Marion Bailey. Each year she would proclaim, "This I the best class I've ever had." Regardless of how the class seemed when the young anxious faces scanned the room for hints of things to come, Marion knew her belief in the potential of this class would shape it into what it could be—her best ever. She was determined to see this group of children as great. It was a tribute to her own greatness as a teacher that she indeed crafted a fantastic class year after year.

Marion, now retired, was not a magician. She understood that her perceptions of children decided who they would become in her classroom and from her choices for their interaction flowed their sense of community and belonging. A cornerstone of her classroom was her belief in the power of community. As she spent time getting to know the children and helping them to know and appreciate each other, she focused on what each one could do and welcomed the opportunity to help them with what they couldn't. In the culture of some schools, this faith in children to work well and care about each other would be considered Pollyanna thinking. It takes commitment and knowing that it works. Year after year Marion patiently proved that it did.

When I returned to the classroom after thirteen years teaching reading in small groups or conferring with writers in other teachers' classrooms, I found the social issues a logjam in the learning momentum. I resented the time spent listening to complaints, sorting through hurt feelings, finding temporary panaceas for problems I knew would crop up again in a matter of days, hours, even minutes. Couldn't we just get on with our learning lives?

No, we couldn't. This *is* life in the classroom where children are free to be themselves and I didn't want to change that. Human differences and habits complicate and challenge the smooth current of the river. Wise colleagues counseled, "Pay close attention to the social curriculum in the beginning of the year. It is even more important than the mandated one." Now I know that the social curriculum and the academic curriculum are like a pair of shoes. Children who walk with only one shoe develop an awkward gait, and I couldn't just pretend that one foot wasn't bare and in jeopardy.

I could not ignore social problems and hope they would go away. I needed to help children with social skills as well as the skills in the academic curriculum. Sometimes their words rubbed against each other until their coping skills were worn to a nub. Mopping up social puddles that spilled over into the classroom may not have been how I wanted to spend my time, but I needed to help the children build relationships with each other that could withstand the intensity of life in the classroom. That wouldn't happen without modeling and practice. Students needed my help as they learned how to interact in ways that made our journey smoother and more productive.

Reading Daniel Goleman's *Emotional Intelligence* alerted me to another reason classroom relationships need to be healthy—they actually affect our physical health.

> One study of college roommates found that the more they disliked each other, the more susceptible they were to colds and the flu, and the more frequently they went to doctors. John Cacioppo, the Ohio State University psychologist who did the roommate study, told me, "It's the most important relationships in your life, the people you see day in and day out, that seem to be crucial for your health." (1995, 179)

As I began to study my class through the lens of relationships, I realized that how the children related to each other was interfering with their ability to learn and grow together. When Brendan teased Ben about his glasses, it wasn't just Ben who was affected. When Josephine shared her markers with Filippa but not with Michele, the whole class felt the reverberation. I needed to spend time on how the children related to each other. It could not be only when the need arose or I would have to carry a fire extinguisher to put out the constant emotional fires. The students needed help with social skills and interactions. I added that to my job description. Once I did, once I accepted that children needed help learning how to get along just like they needed help learning to add and subtract, life in our small space began to improve.

Observing my young learners interact, reading, and talking to colleagues about the importance of the social curriculum, I became convinced that in order to have a well-functioning classroom, children must care about each other. I couldn't just hope that the children would find a few friends in the class. I needed to do my very best to ensure that all children felt valued and included.

I have found three primary ways I can help create a learning environment where everyone feels appreciated, motivated, and productive:

> Acknowledge my role in creating a sense of belonging among the students.
>
> Understand and promote the vital role membership plays in the classroom dynamic.
>
> Celebrate with students the bounty of personal differences.

MY ROLE IN CREATING
A SENSE OF BELONGING

It was almost easier when I was a young, inexperienced teacher. When things didn't go well in the classroom, I blamed the students. They had a problem. After a while I began to realize that my own moods, energy level, expectations, preferences, and personal issues followed me into the classroom each morning. Whether I liked it or not, I had to accept responsibility for the way our daily script played out. My subtle messages, verbal and nonverbal, sent signals to the children that I didn't know I was sending. There was a subtext to our daily communications that I was missing. I wanted to be authentic and real and yet I also wanted to be in charge. What I learned was that first I had to take charge of myself. I had to become the role model for listening and caring and the hardest part was I couldn't fake it.

Children know when adults are pretending to be sincere. A sweet voice and a warm smile will not pass for affection. I had to let go of as much of my personal baggage as possible and focus on each child. As the townwide writing teacher for five years, I spent most of the day conferring with young writers. This daily practice honed my listening skills. It took me a while to stop worrying about giving children the correct responses and just clear my head and trust my understanding of them and of writing. I wanted to listen patiently and intently to their words and register their nonverbal signals. I wasn't the only teacher in the room, so I gave myself permission to ignore everything but the young writers in front of me. I listened to their words and their pauses and the intention and desire behind what they said. As I once heard Mary Ellen Giacobbe say, I listened with such attention "I sucked their words right out of their mouths."

Riveted listening allowed me to learn so much from and about each child and connected us like a lamp plugged into an outlet. Kids lit up in the glow of my intense focus. I wasn't just feigning interest in them and their stories—I was and still am sincerely fascinated by the stories others tell, regardless of their experience as a storyteller. The real benefit was that students felt a renewed connection to their writing and returned to it energized.

These writing conferences showed me what it means to be truly available as a listener. Back in the classroom, even as the only teacher, I know the importance of such intense listening. When children discover their own solutions during our conversations, I know I've listened especially well.

I still have days when I'm preoccupied and know I'm not really paying attention to student responses or questions as well as I'd like to. My responses are superficial and rote. But I've learned that children can help me reconnect to them. I just have to ask. Feeling connected to the class is just as important to the students. I want them to know this satisfying and comfortable feeling. Both teachers and kids play a pivotal role in helping all members feel integral and significant.

Modeling

I set high standards for myself in the classroom. I may not always feel cheery and upbeat, but for the most part, I try to be. Even on the days when I would rather be home in my bathrobe, nursing a scratchy throat with a hot cup of tea, my responsibility is to model being a good group member. When a sinus infection has turned my head into a raging struggle, I let the children in on my little secret, "Boy, do I feel awful today. But I'll try my best to still be patient, kind, and caring. And I'll really appreciate your patience, kindness, and caring." Some children will be able to rise to the occasion, but some will not, just as I may not be all I wish to be in every moment.

The way I treat each child is the way I want children to treat each other. If I am impatient or disrespectful, I can expect to see them treat each other that way. Don't get me wrong, I do not assume full responsibility for their behavior, but on the other hand, I have more power than I may want at times to influence how they act when we are together. I set the tone. If I model caring and appreciation, I have a much better chance of seeing those same behaviors in my students.

I remember an eye-opening lesson taught to me inadvertently by a frustrated colleague. "These kids are so mean to each other!" she stormed during a lunch conversation, her anger oozing into her salad. She would cancel their choice time that afternoon. These children did not deserve time to make choices and play together. What teacher hasn't felt those same feelings and thought those same thoughts?

What most upsets me about that kind of scenario—especially when I am the teacher trapped in the middle of it—is that all too easily mean children beget a mean teacher. When I hear children being mean to each other, it brings out the mean in me. I want to shout at them, "Stop it! Now!" And of course, that is exactly *not* the kind of behavior I want to model.

I am learning to take a deep breath and share my feelings with the children involved. I struggle with the same rush to be unkind that they must be feeling. How can we help each other change the course of our words and actions? Earlier in my teaching career I would have tried to sweep the problem under the rug or lectured the class about kind behavior, but it only left a huge bump for us to trip over again and again. Spending the time on these uncomfortable issues and considering, "What can you do differently next time?" keeps the focus positive and gives children a stronger sense of control. Most importantly, it helps to reconnect students who had been separated by their feelings toward each other, just as my colleague who wanted to cancel choice time needed to reconnect with her students.

Yesterday after lunch recess, chaos stormed through the door along with the overheated and overtired class. I hoped the next event—Lizzie had brought in apples and honey to share for the beginning of the Jewish New Year—would calm everyone down and help them relax. Instead, when Paula dipped her apple slice twice into the honey on the plate they were sharing, Jack called out in alarm, "She double-dipped!"

Bobby picked up the pseudo-panic. "Paula double-dipped!"

Murmurs quickly leapt from table to table. Paula slumped over her arms and dissolved into tears. Like the honey over the apple slices, our celebration slid quickly downhill.

As I observed this small but significant crisis, my end-of-the-week weary mind thought, "Well, we just won't have any celebrations. Who needs this nonsense?" Fortunately my more patient and positive self pushed back that damaging and negative thinking.

"Good heavens! I must be tired," I realized, licking honey off my sticky fingers and taking a deep breath. How do I bring us back into the harmony we need? My image of the class when they are their best morning selves provided the beacon. I trusted that we could find our balance and learn from this incident that caused Paula personal upset. Jack and Bobby had no idea that their observations and comments would result in tears for Paula and a pervasive disequilibrium for the class. The children rightfully looked to the adult in the room to help get their ship back on course.

I held up my slice of apple and quietly asked everyone to look at it. "This is what we are getting upset about . . . a tiny slice of apple with a touch of honey. Isn't it amazing what can make us feel unhappy? I'd love to hear three ways we can help each other get back the good feelings of Lizzie's celebration." After three children shared their ideas, I thanked them and tried to lighten the moment as the children prepared for read aloud time. Jack, Bobby, and Paula needed a quick and private word to help them sort through what had just happened and to focus on how they could handle the situation differently next time. Harmony was restored and we began to feel whole again as I launched into the next exciting chapter of *The Mouse and the Motorcycle* by Beverly Cleary.

These are the teachable moments—the classroom disturbances that we cannot predict and definitely don't want. But they provide the grist for the ever-present social mill. As we take time to talk through issues and model thoughtful strategies for problem solving *with* the children, they experience ways to handle conflict and disappointment that can be added to their repertoire of social skills.

A large, bright yellow sign hangs on the back bulletin board. "Please be kind," it requests. For that colorful sign to have any meaning, I must model kindness every second of the day. I can take down the "Manners Matter" sign if I don't model what they are to do. My repeated "Please" and "Thank you" must be sincere. Perhaps what makes the social curriculum so demanding is that we must model and live what we teach. If we don't, the ways our children interact with each other will continue to feel like we're dragging an anchor.

As I set my intention to model kindness and caring, I want the children to understand that I am but one source of good feeling in the room. They contribute to the well-being of each other. We are cocreators of our balanced and nourishing ecosystem.

Structures and Rituals That Begin on the Very First Day

What is the difference between a structure and a ritual? My definition is a practical one based on experience. A structure is a solid cornerstone of the school day. It is the foundation that secures the rest of the activities by its certainty and importance. Solid as a rock, these elements support the more fluid schedule and give predictability and security. A hurricane may blow through the classroom during recess, but read aloud would go on as expected. Most structures, such as morning meeting, sustained silent reading following morning recess, and read aloud following lunch recess, begin the first day of school.

Rituals are the repeated procedures that add stability and familiarity to the daily routine. Some basic rituals are how we line up, how I get the attention of the class, how we greet each other in the morning. Rituals often evolve as the class discovers patterns that feel right for them. These rituals are practiced daily until they become a resilient thread in the fabric of classroom life. It's so much easier to leave the class with a guest teacher when rituals have become well-accepted habits.

Getting Their Attention

When I decentralize the classroom for optimum participation, I need to be sure I can get everyone's attention back without resorting to a bullhorn. Expectations must be absolutely clear and students must share the responsibility for a prompt response to a signal for attention. I've tried a variety of signals over the years and have found that a foolproof system one year may not work as well with the next year's class. Whatever procedure I set in place, the children need to practice it. I must be consistent and wait until everyone responds to the signal before I proceed. If I raise my hand for their attention and then begin speaking while Mary and Judy are still conferring about a story, I undermine my expectation.

For the past several years I have used a raised hand signal that dictates "Stop, look, listen, and smile." The smile is just to lighten the mood after being interrupted. If we reach a point in the year when my signal seems to be having less impact, we have a brief meeting to talk about why it is important. I also try hard not to interrupt the flow of their work time any more than absolutely necessary. Like most adults, children hate to be interrupted in the middle of a project. Unfortunately, the rhythm of the school day often makes it unavoidable. Since the daily routine depends on smooth transitions from one activity to the next, I gladly donate time for children to understand the importance of stopping on cue and for role-playing and practicing how to do it well.

Every year I struggle with one or two children who resist joining the group effort. A private, gentle word with these recalcitrant few usually solves the problem as they see how their commitment to the group matters to everyone. For the children who have yet to experience the satisfaction of belonging to a winning team, the demands of cooperation may seem a steep price to pay. Nevertheless, I want them to know that their participation is important to the group and ask them to do the best they can. Often as their connection to me and to the group strengthens, so does their willingness to follow group rules and norms. I want to organize the day and class as best I can to accommodate everyone in the group. My goal cannot be to fix kids so they will simply comply with a long list of rules. My goal is that they confidently and willingly manage their own behavior. I have found that internal controls, learned slowly over time, beat external controls every time.

One year, Bruce only looked up when other children raised their hands at the quiet signal. His attitude appeared defiant and challenging. I knew I had to disarm this warhead. A residue of misunderstandings had followed him from his previous school experiences and from his family life. Bruce was giving me a strong and clear message that he needed to feel special and important to the class. Over the next few weeks I scurried to discover his strengths. He helped assemble a bookcase that arrived. He held the cord while I walked around the room videotaping. He cleaned out the hamster cage with Jessica. As he grew to trust his classmates and me, he slowly began to comply with expectations. When it was his turn to be "person of the day," he politely insisted that all children give him their attention before he called tables to morning meeting. Bruce eventually became such a reliable class member that I almost forgot who he had been when the year had started. Often, the kids who resist involvement in the group are the ones who crave it the most. Their fear of rejection or a repetition of unsuccessful social patterns inhibits their ability to even try. For me, these lessons present a more challenging problem than how to teach children regrouping in addition or how to write an interesting lead. Since our prisons are filled with inmates who can add but can't get along in society, I know these social and emotional issues are the toughest lessons for many in school and in life.

Subdividing

The social structure of the room can fall apart if teacher expectations are not clear and understood. After fifteen years as a teacher of small groups or working in someone else's classroom, I had rather naïve notions about what was needed to help children move smoothly around the room, into line, and from activity to activity. I can see myself smiling at the eager, young, second-grade children and telling them to quietly get in line. I had forgotten about the need to subdivide the class to make routines manageable.

Of course, twenty-two second graders raced across the room to be first in line. Little did I know that place in line was like social rank in Victorian England. Number nine in line was much more important than number ten. "Cutting" in line was also a big issue.

As much as I didn't want to take the time to call the students by tables, colors, alphabet, whatever, it was necessary to avoid chaos and hurt feelings. By subdividing the group as they lined up or went back to their seats from the learning circle, I spared them the uncertainty they felt when disorder ensued. I learned to quietly call children into line one small bundle at a time so they didn't have to get upset with their classmates for crowding. Subdividing lubricates the classroom flow and calms potentially squeaky wheels.

Provisioning

Having needed supplies at the ready is another rule of thumb I quickly relearned. Fumbling through the paper cupboard for orange construction paper the week before Halloween is to invite Darren to fall off his chair or Emma to call across to Megan to borrow her crayons. When the supplies, worksheets, paints, and other supplies are ready and waiting, I prevent children from slipping into the tiny behaviors that annoy their peers. If I am prepared and ready, the momentum is maintained and potential social problems are avoided.

Does it sound like my class is ever-vigilant, waiting for a moment's pause to fill it with chaos? No, not usually. But by provisioning properly I help children feel safe and comfortable. When the unexpected does happen—and of course, it always does ("Mrs. Skolnick, the handle fell off the pencil sharpener.")—the reliance on routines supports us. Disagreeable behavior between students can be short-circuited by careful planning and preparation.

Seating Arrangements

The way children interact also depends on the classroom seating arrangements. Are there spaces in the room where partners or small groups can work quietly? Are there solitary spaces where a child can work undisturbed? One study of successful classrooms found that children work best when there are nooks and crannies for them to use. Like our hamster, Ralph, children need places to curl up and get away from it all.

Seating at tables or desks can inhibit or promote camaraderie. Groups or tables of four seem to maximize group interaction without overwhelming the child who prefers a smaller social setting. One caveat cannot be stressed enough: Groups must remain fluid. Seating arrangements that become carved in stone are deadly to a healthy classroom environment. Two or three weeks at a table seems to be optimum. Each time the children draw cards and move to a new table, a fresh dynamic is set into place. There is a new opportunity to get to know classmates on a more intimate level. As children work together, exchanging ideas and information, their understanding and knowledge of each other grows.

One cold winter day a former student stopped by for a visit. "Do you know what's the hardest thing about this year?" she asked me. "We never change seats! I'm sitting with the same kids that I did the first week of school. They're really starting to get on my nerves." I laughed with Emma as she described the irritating behavior that she tried to tolerate. It was clear from her detailed description of their habits that a change of scenery was in order.

In adult life we are asked to work with others regardless of personal preferences. I ask the same of the children in my class. Yes, Cybil can work at the same table as Walter, even if he does forget and hum random tunes. But she doesn't have to sit there for more than two weeks. And there are other places in the room where she can seek sanctuary during independent work times. She can also learn more about Walter—for instance, that he's a kind and artistic person, and his humming helps him concentrate. It may feel less intrusive when she understands he does it naturally, not as a planned annoyance. Children are more willing to sit at tables not of their choice when they know it's for a limited time.

Periodically I ask the students to rate themselves as a table mate. First we agree on what makes a good table mate. Last year the class reference chart read, I am a good table mate if I . . .

1. help keep center bin organized
2. keep my things in my blue folder
3. don't comment out loud and I just do it
4. help others at my table with cleaning up
5. listen to the person speaking
6. follow directions that help my table
7. am not distracted by talking to friends
8. treat others at the table with kindness

Once we established our expectations for behavior at the table, I typed up a graph so they could color in their rating of themselves for each category on a scale of one to four. As they colored in the graph, it gave them an opportunity to reflect on their contribution to the success and comfort level at their table.

Our classroom also has a carpeted space where we can sit together in a circle or rows. The movement from the tables to the carpet shifts the energy and allows children necessary movement. During read aloud, sustained silent reading, and other more flexible times, children may choose whether to sit at their table or work on the floor or at another table or countertop. The configurations of partners is fairly fluid as children make decisions about who to sit next to during these quiet, relaxed times. Ben may pull a chair up next to mine and finger knit as I read aloud from *The Castle in the Attic* by Elizabeth Winthrop. Charles and Nick may sit with Jason at the long table and share a basket of markers. Gabriella and Paige may stretch out next to each other on the floor, listening intently as they color in a birthday wish. Jake sits alone at his table, staring straight ahead, mesmerized by the tale of enchantment. The freedom to chose their spot in the room during these special times adds to the feeling of community. The gently shifting arrangement each day as the children position themselves to read silently or listen to the read aloud also gives me valuable data about the classroom climate.

THE VITAL ROLE OF MEMBERSHIP

In the classroom, with its bounty of differences, there is one common denominator: Everyone needs to belong. When children sense that they are separate from the group, their behavior takes a variety of counterproductive avenues. William wanders around the edge of the group nudging other children. He doesn't know how to feel like part of the group. Kathy sets up house back in the corner, building a nest with her special things. But it's not a special nest that Kathy is seeking. It's friendship. Her separation from the group is a defensive move. Some children attract other kids to them and easily make connections. Others don't know how to initiate a friendship and certainly don't have the know-how yet to sustain one. These are the children who need that sense of connection the most, and who need to learn how to relate to their classmates in ways that are positive and caring.

Recently I met with Kathy's therapist. As we talked about how I could best work with Kathy, she brought this issue into clearer focus.

"Kathy really wants a best friend," she told me. "That's how she measures her success in school. It's not about academics. In first grade she wasn't invited to one play date. She felt like a complete failure."

I didn't doubt what this skilled therapist told me. The pleasure of school and learning is diminished for children with social concerns. Their academic growth takes a backseat to their feelings of social inadequacy. This verified what I had read in an article in the *New York Times* a decade ago that stated social issues in school can inhibit learning. Kids outside the social circle by third grade begin to fall off their learning curve. For some children, it no doubt happens even before third grade. When children feel unaccepted, they lose their learning momentum.

Helping children learn the social skills to be a good group member needs to be a priority. These are skills with lifelong value. I also want to help children improve their social skills for selfish reasons—the quality of our daily life improves. But there is even a bigger reason: children's lives hang in the balance. Kids who are marginalized in school feel disconnected from the group. Their perception of separateness permits them to ignore group norms and responsibilities. Sometimes their behavior is attention-seeking, such as when Mark draws colorful tattoos on his arm with markers, or defiant, as when Nathan refuses to come to the morning meeting, or poor sportsmanship, as when Robert ends each recess red-faced and angry with his classmates. A sense of belonging and being of consequence is a salve on life's wounds.

You Can't Say You Can't Play

A book that influenced my view of classroom life is *You Can't Say You Can't Play* by Vivian Gussin Paley (1992). Her insightful book begins this way:

> Turning sixty, I am more aware of the voices of exclusion in the classroom. "You can't play" suddenly seems too overbearing and harsh, resounding

like a slap from wall to wall. How casually one child determines the fate of another. (1)

I am not a teacher who believes in imposing random rules on the class. After reading the book I thought I'd be democratic and let the children vote on whether or not they wanted "you can't say you can't play" to be a class rule. Of course, they would vote in favor of it. However, after an elaborate and unexpected lobbying effort by a handful of girls, the rule was defeated.

It took me less than a week to realize I could not sanction the exclusion it permitted. The final straw was when the Brownie Troop leader told me the girls in my class quoted me: "Mrs. Skolnick said it was all right if we told someone we didn't want to play with them."

The next morning I called the class to the learning circle and told them I had been wrong to put such an important rule to a vote. It felt too unkind. I used my executive privilege and reversed their decision. I could sense a collective sigh of relief. Since then I've introduced the rule, not as an option, but with an opportunity to talk about why it is best for everyone if we live by the words "you can't say you can't play."

The children need time to process and explore what those words mean as they are lived out during recess, choice time, and other unstructured times. I ask them to consider what the words feel like when they are inside the social group and what the words feel like when they are on the outside looking in. Discussions about their meaning and implications are essential to a clear understanding of how the class will function as a group, what is acceptable treatment, and what we can expect of each other. Repeated conversations about the purpose and exceptions are necessary for the rule to take root, but each year I'm relieved when I see it in action. And thank heavens for the Jackies, the Davids, and the Sophies who gently but firmly take a stand during free play to insist the rule be followed. I am grateful to the handful of children with a heightened sense of moral justice who go out on the limb with their classmates and keep the rule alive. I am also grateful to Vivian Paley for her wisdom. Her insights helped me find another way to help children feel a sense of membership.

Using Specific Language

I know I'm not in top form when my thinking and language becomes global: "Nobody is listening. Everyone is wasting time." My brain skips right past the kids who are on task and busy learning and dwells on those who are not. I nudge myself back on track and sometimes ask the class for assistance. "Help me," I've learned to say. "I'm feeling like no one is listening. I need the kids who are listening to pat themselves on the back [nod their heads, flap their wings, and so on] so I can focus on who's doing it right." This quick maneuver indicates who is paying attention and I can shift gears if necessary. Often it is all it takes to remind students to focus and to keep me positive.

When children are upset, they often slip into global language, too. "Everybody hates me" or "Nobody will play with me" on closer inspection means that one or two children will not play or are angry with them. Helping kids learn to translate that into more specific language can defuse "Everybody hates me" into "Sarah's mad at me." The feeling may be just as intense, but the problem becomes more manageable. The language we use creates our world. I want children to shape their world in more gentle and yielding terms. Making them aware of how they use language in everyday situations can strengthen and clarify their thinking and help them rebound from a sense of disaster.

I try to be sensitive to the same global/specific issue when I notice what children are doing well. I want them to be able to do that again, so the more precisely I can describe their success, the better their chance of repeating it. "Nice job!" in the margin of Michael's journal will not be as useful "I can see this so clearly! Great description!" Or "I love your strong verbs!"

I squirm in my chair when a parent tells me how his child quotes me at home. What "Mrs. Skolnick said . . . " will hopefully be somewhat accurate. What makes it daunting is that some children take our words so seriously. I want those words to help them grow and flourish. In our book *On Their Way: Celebrating Second Graders as They Read and Write* (1994), Jane Fraser and I call listening and talking the power tools in the classroom. The way we talk with children influences the way they talk with each other. If children hear me constantly giving reminders to Jon, it is not long before Jon feels separate from the group. My words and nonverbal messages can create either a sense of inclusion or a withering sense of exclusion.

One bleak February day I confessed to my trusted friend and peer coach, Anne Nesbitt, that a child in my class was starting to fray my nerves. Ian's parents were going through a sudden and unexpected divorce. His world had crumbled and his response to this personal devastation was to be expected—he regressed. At any imagined slight he dissolved into tears, curling up distraught in the corner. I understood why he was acting this way and I knew he was coping the best he could, but after several weeks, I was uncomfortable with my internal response to Ian's behavior. With time and help he would get through this very real life crisis, but meanwhile, I was letting it drain me. I also knew that the very last thing Ian needed was an impatient teacher who wanted him to stop acting like a baby. The other children would quickly pick up on this message, change their behavior toward him, and Ian's sense of despair would only increase.

So I invited Anne in during reading to play Sherlock Holmes. Could she detect which child was taxing my patience? Was I sending unintentional negative signals? As Anne watched, I read *Solomon, the Rusty Nail* to the rapt William Steig fans. We discussed how the book was like his other books and the children dispersed to read on their own.

I looked at Anne. She shook her head. She couldn't spot the child in question. My responses to Ian's comments had not been laced with cyanide, after all. I took a deep breath. If my colleague with a built-in sensor for anti-kid behavior didn't register a difference, hopefully Ian and the rest of the class couldn't either. Now I just needed to work on renewing my connection to him and helping him develop a support system and strategies to get him through this painful time.

My attentive listening and thoughtful responses encourage similar interaction. Something as simple as "wait time" assures more probing interactions. The rhythm and tone of my language sets the scene in the classroom. If I want children to be thoughtful and patient with each other, guess who must be the most thoughtful and patient?

CELEBRATING THE
BOUNTY OF DIFFERENCES

On the teacher workday before school began last fall, four of us were still lingering over our sodas and filling each other in on our summers. "We had a great family summer," Margaret reported. "But I worry about my daughter, Gina. At eleven, she's such an individual. I worry that she's different."

Anne Nesbitt smiled at Margaret. "All children are different," she said gently.

I laughed out loud—one of those embarrassing chortles. In four simple words Anne had spelled out one of the basic truths about classroom life: *All children are different.* It is a fact of human nature and yet, in the insidious pull toward conformity in schools, we often act like this is a surprise. If we could keep these four simple words in mind our schools would be better places for children. That all children are as unique as snowflakes melts away in the heat of the daily classroom rush. Appreciating differences starts with Anne's reminder. And what a treasure it is that children come in such an assortment of humanness.

Accepting Versus Tolerating

A year ago I decided I wanted to loop with my class to third grade. After seven years at second grade I was ready to return to third grade. I thought long and hard about it, read the paltry literature available on looping, and talked to teachers who had gone up a grade level with and without their classes. One of my colleagues, Maria Castelluccio, had moved from third to fourth grade the previous year, but had not looped. Therefore, only five of her third-grade students moved up with her. She convinced me that looping made more sense.

"The other twenty kids still aren't sure why they weren't picked to be in my class again. It's hard for them to understand how placement works," she told me.

I knew I couldn't choose five of my class and let the others wonder why they had not been chosen. With more determination than ever, I approached my principal, Dan Sullivan. Dan, who ordinarily was so positive and supportive, listened to my reasons for wanting to loop, then gave me his reasons why he thought looping was not such a good idea. Finally he said, "It seems that ten months is about the length of time we have with kids before they start getting on our nerves. They also start getting on each other's nerves. Think about whether you can tolerate some of their behaviors for another school year."

Of course, I knew what Dan meant. The countdown at the end of the school year isn't just about summer coming. It's also about saying adios to some children who have demanded so much of our patience and stamina. I had great respect for Dan's opinions, but I had to disagree. This conversation pushed me to grasp the difference between tolerating and accepting.

When I tolerate behaviors in the classroom, I would rather change them. Since I can't really change the child, I try to put up with whatever it is until the end of the school year. But tolerating is a pretense and only leads to exhaustion. Accepting is a whole other ball game. When I accept children for who and how they are I've gone beyond tolerating to understanding and appreciating them. Jenny may forget and call out during class discussions, but I know it's because she's an eager extrovert who thinks out loud. Josh may forget and lie down in the learning circle, but he works with the occupational therapist and is learning to monitor his body better. They are not misbehaving. This is natural. Jenny's enthusiasm gets the best of her. Josh has made important progress. Something that seems so simple, such as sitting quietly in a circle, is as demanding for him as one hundred push-ups would be for me.

Accepting means taking to heart children with all their foibles. I'm still working to help them be cooperative and engaged class members, but I'm not spending energy wishing they would change. This is who they are. This is how they are.

Later, as I was pondering this notion, my sister Karen called from Houston.

"We were just out for a thirty-mile bike ride," she announced. "It was great!"

"How do you do it?" I asked. I wouldn't want to walk to the mailbox in their heat and humidity.

"Oh, we start early. It doesn't get much above 95 degrees before we finish."

I needed a cool shower just having this conversation. I'm allergic to heat. A week of that three-H weather and I'm moaning and complaining. After eight years in Houston, Karen has gracefully accepted the weather. It's no big deal. I can tolerate that hot, sticky air for a few days, but then it starts to wear me out. Like the teacher with a tedious child at the end of the year, I'll complain to anyone who will listen. I doubted I could ever learn to accept such weather conditions on a regular basis. About all I could manage was to tolerate the week or two of the high heat and humidity that strikes each summer. Then I just want it to go away.

After all this consideration, I *did* loop with my class. The amazing part for me was how my affection for the children grew as the second year progressed. They taught me an important lesson in accepting. I didn't come undone every time Josh lay down in the learning circle. I could make an instantaneous decision that Josh was better off lying down at that moment or flash Jenny a quick nonverbal reminder when she called out her pressing idea. I would have taken every one of those children on to fourth grade. I knew who they were and they knew me. We became a great team.

My challenge is to take that lovely lesson on to the next class: *Know and appreciate who they are and accept the whole package.* When I stop judging good or bad and appreciate and celebrate what is, the crashing waves turn into a lapping tide. Without resistance on my part to who and how they are, we are freer to grow together.

Accepting differences among the children is easier for me now that I understand that many of their styles and preferences are hardwired. In the past several years I've been fascinated by the different learning styles, multiple intelligences, and personality preferences that the children bring to school. As I've studied the Myers-Briggs Personality Types and the work of Howard Gardner with multiple intelligences, I've come to grasp the many possible ways we approach learning and life. It has helped me be more forgiving of my own shortcomings, as well. For example, I am perpetually late returning library books. No matter how hard I try, I have yet to perfect the art of returning all the many books I check out on time. This would be enough to cause some librarians to rip up my bar code, but fortunately the good-natured women at the local library collect my fines with a smile. I appreciate that they don't feel the need to play historian with me and remind me of all the times in the past when I also had books or tapes overdue. No, they accept my imperfection along with my cash and I don't have to waste emotional energy on feeling guilty. I would probably find another library if I had to skulk in each time to disparaging and impatient looks. How grateful I am for their non-judgmental acceptance.

When I can appreciate children for who and how they are, even if at times they may appear as a zircon in the rough, I am fulfilling one of their fundamental psychological needs. On the PBS television show *The Seven Spiritual Laws of Success,* Deepak Chopra listed these three qualities as essential to our psychological well-being: *attention, acceptance,* and *appreciation.* I see these as a continuum. The simplest need is for attention. As any teacher knows, children will go to unbelievable lengths to have this need met. From the superachiever to the underachiever to the class clown, it is an essential human force to desire attention.

But for attention to feel gratifying it needs to be linked to acceptance, a higher order psychological need. Attention that does not include acceptance is like the night without stars. We sense something is missing. The highest order, appreciation, surpasses both attention and acceptance. It adds a full moon to the night sky. When someone appreciates what I do, that is the pinnacle of attention and acceptance.

What does this mean in the classroom? How does a teacher appreciate the students, not just give them her positive regard as attention and acceptance, but truly appreciate who they are and their contribution? An even more challenging question is how does a teacher help the children to accept and appreciate each other?

"We like what we know," claims an old adage. With children, they like what they know, what they understand, what makes sense. Their ability to appreciate each other rests on their ability to know and understand each other in ways that allow them to feel safe and comfortable together. Most importantly, when their own primary needs are met, they are more generous in their acceptance and appreciation of each other.

Accepting and appreciating differences requires a nonjudgmental stance. Teachers guide children as they learn and grow but our mission is not to mold each one into the perfect scholarly package.

When I was an elementary student in the 1950s, there seemed to be one kind of model student. The rules for success were many and membership into the perfecto kiddo club was limited. Star charts on classroom walls honored the excellent spellers and those quick with multiplication facts. Reading groups loudly proclaimed the names of the top dog readers. An academic hierarchy pervaded and poisoned the environment.

I loved it! It worked for me. I could bark out the right words and the right facts on cue. And I certainly wasn't concerned about the kids who hovered on the lower rung of the academic ladder. In my scramble for personal reward, I ignored those for whom school was a daily chore. I thought the music played for everyone. Why weren't they dancing? I didn't understand that we decipher the information we receive differently and that we don't even all receive the same information.

This elitist attitude toward school was bred deep in my bones at home, at school, and in society. It's taken me years to shake it, and in moments of stress, I feel the pull of conformity, the flagship of schools. But now alarm bells go off in my head. If only the best songbirds sang, the forest would be quiet.

The model I want to embrace in my classroom comes from nature with its glorious acceptance of variety. If that is my compass, I can guide the young lives who share my day into a wider perspective of how the world works. We are all invited to the party. We can all dance, sing, clap, stomp, or do whatever we do best to experience and enjoy the rhythms of life. This more expansive and generous view of children appreciates their mistakes and imperfections as part of the plan. Maybe not my original plan, but the one that is unfolding. In this way, I can allow for the very best from every young life I touch.

Expecting that the children in my class treat each other with care and compassion may seem like planting a daffodil in the desert. Even some experienced adults in the United States Congress appear to lack these qualities. How can I have such high standards for children?

How can I not? But habits develop slowly—I must be willing to invest time for modeling and practice if I want children to have habits of goodness. Together we must have the continual conversations about friendship and thoughtfulness. It's not incidental to the day. It's what makes each day feel worthwhile.

In the fifties of my childhood, fostering supportive relationships and collaboration among students was as unheard of as reading workshop instead of reading groups. Friendships between and among students happened in the neighborhood or on the playground. Once the bell rang, relationships were restricted to nonverbal signals or passing notes. "Leave your life at the door" should have been the sign over the tall archway of Washington Elementary School. Educators didn't know then that inviting in real children with real lives, worries, imaginations, and curiosities and helping them to harness all that natural energy into healthy relationships with each other and the curriculum would enrich the school.

CHAPTER 5 SUGGESTS A NUMBER OF WAYS TO HELP CHILDREN GET TO know each other better. Through structured and informal interactions, children grow in their respect for each other, emulating the respect and reverence shown to them by their teacher.

5

Developing a Sense of Membership

As I write this chapter, I'm thinking about Peter, whose deepest wish was to have a best friend. I'm thinking about Josey, who needed recognition so desperately she would rub her skin until it was red and raw, then ask to go to the nurse. I'm thinking of David, with such high goals for himself that he chewed the front of his T-shirt, leaving a large wet circle all the way down to the Yankees logo. I'm thinking of the kids who sit patiently in their seats each day waiting for school to be over. I'm writing this chapter for those kids, because I know we can make their school lives better with a shift in our focus and a change in some of our well-worn classroom habits.

This chapter invites you to look at your classroom through the eyes of your students. Regardless of all the exciting lessons and activities you plan and organize, their sense of satisfaction depends on their interactions with the other students and their belief that they are of consequence in the learning community. We are not teaching to computer-like brains that learn in spite of the emotional tenor. The way children relate to each other in the classroom impacts directly on their ability to learn and grow.

Whenever humans get together, whether to learn, solve thorny issues, or take responsibility for change, personalities impose on the process. This happens each day in the classroom. Teachers negotiate around and through the needs of twenty-five different individuals with different life experiences, different personality preferences, different learning styles, and different needs and goals.

The traditional and unsuccessful way to deal with all of this was to put a lid on it. If everyone just stays seated, busy, and quiet we can pretend none of these issues are lurking right below the surface. Children are the most human of people, and ignoring social concerns does a terrific injustice to their development. They have varied and full lives. Small in stature does not mean small in concerns or emotional issues. The way their lives intersect determines the academic and emotional health of classrooms.

This chapter features activities that help kids learn how to relate better to each other, one of the most challenging responsibilities we have as teachers. The ideas I offer are borrowed from some of the finest classrooms and fine-tuned in my own. They are not necessarily new, but they offer a fresh twist that emphasizes children connecting to children. They may seem too simple to make a difference, yet they do. All contribute to the sense of belonging that is the cornerstone of classroom effectiveness. They also create a sense of interdependence and an awareness of the importance of working together for everyone to do their best. Cooperation replaces competition.

I have ten basic ground rules that I apply to the activities beyond their obvious contribution to learning. For these group activities to be worthy of our time, they will:

1. increase the sense of membership and belonging

2. involve everyone

3. require doing or cocreating

4. allow for a variety of configurations of students working together

5. allow kids to enter at their own comfort level

6. offer a degree of choice

7. be nonthreatening to the students (and the teacher)

8. provide a safety net so everyone can succeed

9. be worth repeating

10. have a purpose and a lighter side—leave spaces for fun and light-heartedness

Numerous activities may fit the above descriptors, and in this chapter are some that have proven successful over time for me and colleagues. I've divided my suggestions into three categories:

- rituals and structures to put in place ASAP

- activities that help children get to know each other early in the year

- activities that can be used throughout the year to keep relationships strong and nourished

RITUALS AND STRUCTURES
TO PUT IN PLACE ASAP

Morning Meeting

Morning meeting starts the first morning of the new school year once the children have had a chance to settle in. (For more details of this important ritual, please see Chapter 3 and the literature from the Northeast Foundation for Children [Charney 1992; Strachota 1996; Wood 1994].) There are a variety of ways to start the day together that make everyone feel visible and valued. Morning meeting is predictable, but with enough variety to keep it interesting. This ten to fifteen minutes each morning after the bell rings sets the tone and invites everyone to be a part of the day ahead.

Transition Activities

I have found little ways to add zip to transition times and to help myself be more patient during those times when all I want kids to do is get their things put away and come to the learning circle. How hard could that be? Well, with all the details of their busy lives just waiting to be discussed, there are times it can take a lot longer than my patience. So I distract myself and engage those who are ready by clapping a pattern often heard at football games. It goes like this:

Clap, clap, clap-clap-clap, clap-clap-clap, let's go!

The children who are ready clap the pattern clap three times with me and the third time we say, "Let's stop!" They enjoy the movement and rhythm and my impatience dissolves as I clap and chant along with the class. Those who were straggling over to our circle start to hustle and we usually have everyone by the time we get to "Let's stop!" My previous choice would have been to nag individual children, albeit pleasantly, to get moving. The class chant, with its catchy beat, attracts children to the group like a magnet and builds a sense of belonging.

Another technique I use rather than personal reminders at transition times is to start singing this little song:

Please have a seat.
Please have a seat.
No more talking,
No more walking.
Please have a seat.

The first two lines and the last line match the beginning of "Three Blind Mice." Both middle lines are sung at the same note with the second line going up one note for the four beats.

I may not sing this simple song every day, but when time is tight and I need everyone back at their tables, the class quickly joins in and scurries back to sit down. Singing a song together, even one so mundane, adds a new flavor to the moment. I would rather sing than complain about our snail's pace. The children would rather sing than hear a strident voice reminding them, again, that they are going to be late to gym.

The hand-jive is another way to refocus the group. When we're in the learning circle and not everyone has had a turn, but I sense many children are losing their ability to attend, the hand-jive is a quick and lighthearted way to get back on track. "We're going to take a quick hand-jive break," I'll announce. "Let's do it three times, getting faster each time." Kids love that pattern from the play *Grease* and also love to race against the clock, so this grabs their interest and the hand-jive movements feel good. By the time we've done this once or maybe twice, the group is ready to give their attention back to the speaker. This small, fun physical pattern gets us back on track and I don't have to use negative reminders to the kids who had reached the limits of their attention span.

Poems that we have memorized are also great for transitions. Last year my class loved saying Jack Prelutsky's "Homework." We had the words on a large chart back by the learning circle. As the children walked back to the circle, they would recite the poem. Our goal was to have everyone in the circle before we all chanted the final "Homework, oh, homework, I hate you! You stink!" Kids get drawn into the rhythm of the poem and willingly end their conversations. Songs they enjoy singing can also aid movement throughout the room. My class this year has learned to sing a patriotic song on their way back to morning meeting.

Songs, clapping patterns, poems, and chants are ways I have found to keep my focus positive. Rather than repeatedly remind specific children that they need to get with the program, a quick activity lightens our mood and reinforces our sense of belonging. Nagging individual students spreads a sense of dissatisfaction and dissonance. Singing and chanting reconnects us with a positive energy and good feeling.

Person of the Day

I pilfered the idea of person of the day from colleagues when I decided I could use an assistant in the room. I also realized its potential for the students. They rotate through this position according to a large class list on the wall. The duties of person of the day vary from classroom to classroom, but one job in my class is to share some of the responsibility for herding the class at transition times. The child in charge calls children to the circle or into the line by table or other groupings. This relieves me of that task and gives each child an opportunity for leadership. An additional benefit is that each child gets to experience firsthand what it is like to try to get everyone quiet and ready.

Another responsibility of the person of the day in my room is to fill in a large laminated chart that reads:

Person of the Day: _____

Morning Song: _____

Morning Meeting Greeting: _____

Class Pattern: _____

Morning Meeting Activity: _____

Days of School So Far: _____

Days of School Remaining: _____

The person of the day chooses the patriotic song we sing after the pledge, the greeting we use during morning meeting, the pattern that we add to the class pattern, and the game or activity we play in the morning meeting. When the morning bell rings, he asks everyone to rise for the pledge, and after the pledge and song are finished calls the tables back to morning meeting. At other times during the day, he will call the tables to get in line for specials like art or music, or assist me if there is a special job I need done that isn't on the "Job Chart." As the year progresses, I add to the responsibilities of the person of the day. They become the answer person, filling in missed information for children who may have had a momentary shutdown during directions. Sometimes as we go through the rotation of names, they will also be responsible for sharing a favorite poem during morning meeting or at the end of the day share. Occasionally the class decides on new responsibilities for person of the day, and this becomes a new ritual.

Being person of the day invites each child to step into a leadership role. I'm continually surprised to watch the different personas that emerge as students take on the mantle of authority, especially when a shy child becomes assertive and speaks out with a more commanding voice. It also tells me what I sound like as the children address the class in their pseudo-teacher role.

ACTIVITIES THAT HELP CHILDREN
GET TO KNOW EACH OTHER EARLY ON

The relationships between and among the students are nourished by a steady flow of relevant information. Kids need to be interacting in meaningful ways to get to know and appreciate each other. This quote from *Leadership and the New Science* pinpoints why children sharing information is critical to the emotional health of the classroom. "In fact, information is an organization's primary source of nourishment; it is so vital to survival that its absence creates a strong vacuum. If information is not available, people make it up" (Wheatley 1994, 107). When children are responsible for finding out specific information from each other, it generates energy and vitality. They learn more about each other and in the process feel more alert and alive as they gather their data. Active participation is vital during the first few weeks of school, but continues to help create interest and needed information about the students as they learn and grow together throughout the year. The activities are planned specifically so children mingle and talk about the curriculum and their lives.

Student Graphs

Students are invited to meet their teachers during a one-hour open house the day before school begins. This year I decided to help the children find out about each other on their very first visit to the classroom.

Before the kids and their nervous parents arrived to check out the room and Mrs. Skolnick, I hung large charts around the room. I usually have trouble juggling my "hellos" to a number of new faces at one time, so I decided to ask the children to fill in some information about themselves on the charts. Here are some of the questions I asked:

- My teacher last year was _____. (I had a column for each second-grade teacher in our school and a column labeled "other" for kids new to the school.)
- In my family there are _____ children. (I had columns from one to five.)
- My favorite subject last year was _____. (I had a column for reading, writing, math, social studies, and science.)
- My favorite special was _____. (I had a column for art, music, computer, library, and gym.)
- My favorite season is _____. (I had four columns, with summer, fall, winter, and spring.)
- A favorite summer memory is _____. (I listed my name at the top of one column and wrote down a favorite memory in the second column.)

Children who did not come to the open house filled in the charts as everyone was settling in the next morning.

I hung the charts across the chalkboard and used them for our first math lesson. I asked the children to study the charts and discover three things about our class from the information on the charts. Next, I asked them to walk around the room with their clipboards and swap three ideas with other students so their list would grow to six discoveries. This swapping of ideas meant that students had to talk and listen to each other. The listening aspect is key— children who can listen to what classmates are saying are open to learning about them and coming to appreciate who they are.

Before I started this segment of the lesson I modeled the polite way to address each other as they did their swapping:

- Make eye contact to be sure they have the attention of the other student.
- Speak in a quiet but clear voice.
- Ask, "Would you please trade ideas with me?"

I wanted this part of the lesson to be crystal clear. My intention was to have everyone comfortably participating in an exchange of information, not roaming around the room calling out questions or feeling lost.

After I modeled how to address each other, I asked two children to role-play how to speak to each other as they swap ideas. Next I asked for three things the performers did right—further reinforcement for how to speak with each other while gathering data—something the children will be doing a lot during the year. This all takes time, but it is setting the stage for many days of interacting in kind and appropriate ways. This simple format:

- model
- role-play
- responses to what was done right

makes my expectations explicit. The next time I ask the class to gather information, I may do a quick reference chart (see Chapter 3) so that the expectations are on a wall chart as a reminder. My goal is to have the ritual and polite way of interacting become natural.

Once the children have studied the charts and swapped ideas, the lesson ends with sharing what we have learned about each other. I write their statements about our class (e.g., "Most kids like winter the best.") on chart paper. Depending on the interest of the class, this activity can be extended or used as a reminder of the delicious differences that make the class special. An easy and worthwhile follow-up is turning the kids loose the next day to ask their own survey questions. It gives them further practice in talking to each other and learning names.

During the first few weeks of community building I give the students repeated opportunities to discover their similarities and differences. My goal is to help them celebrate and see the value in both.

People Bingo

My colleague Wendy Murphy taught me this simple game for the first day of school. It's another excellent activity for getting kids up out of their seats and interacting. The only materials needed are a clipboard (or a portable hard surface) and a worksheet for each child with a table of empty boxes. Their task is to get the autograph of every person in the room in one of the bingo boxes. With younger children, I've made the empty bingo board with only sixteen boxes so they have fewer signatures to collect. Older children like trying to have everyone sign their bingo sheet. If the class has an uneven number of kids, they can add "free" spaces.

Once they have had a chance to get everyone's autograph and to see what it feels like to be Mark McGwire the year he hit seventy home runs, it's time to play People Bingo. It's just like regular bingo, except as the caller, I am calling out the names of the children in the class. Students try to be the first to cover or cross out an entire row or column of names. The first three big winners get their names on the board and the game starts again. Children want to play over and over—until they win. For those long afternoons the first week of school, People Bingo gets kids up and moving in an organized and purposeful way as they get to know each other.

Sharing Their Pictures

The letter I send to the children prior to the opening of school asks them to bring three things the first day: a healthy snack, a favorite book, and a photo or sketch of a summer memory. These last two items are additional resources for helping the children get to know each other.

For the children who do not have a photograph from the summer, a sketch or drawing captures their memory just as well. First the students share their picture using the questioning format of morning meeting news (see Chapter 3). They tell one sentence about their picture and then call on three to five students who ask questions. This is an easy way to practice the format of news that will become a basic part of morning meeting, and children can find out the information that matters most to them.

Next, the children write a brief description of the picture and these go on the bulletin board along with the picture. This simple activity lets children

- learn about each other
- practice the news format of sharing with the class

- have an opportunity to lead a mini-discussion where they are the expert
- help give me information about their oral and written skills
- fill bulletin boards with relevant and interesting information with little expenditure of time

Sharing Favorite Books

Sharing favorite books can be as simple or elaborate as student interest and time allows. For the children who forget to bring books, they choose a book they know and love from the class library. I explain to children that I will not be reading each book aloud. Rather, we will use their books to learn about each other as readers and to learn about good books.

The learning circle is the setting for this first book share. Children hold their books and in turn tell the class the title, author, and why they choose this book. Then we do a quick class graph of what kinds of books we like to read (sports, mystery, jokes, and so forth). Next I divide the class into groups of two and the children share their book or part of it with this reading partner.

The next assignment with the book may be a response sheet. Before they get to work, we talk about what they've said about their books and brainstorm a list of what they could draw or write on their response sheet. The early lists often include:

- why it's a favorite book
- a favorite part and why
- a character description
- what the book is about

This reference chart stays on the wall and grows as the children grow in their thinking about what they can write about the books they are reading. Sharing their response sheets in the learning circle at the end of reading sends a clear message that their work is important.

A few other activities teachers have done with favorite books are:

- Pairing the children to partner read a favorite part. My colleague Nancy Kovacic does this over a number of days until the children have had a chance to share their book with every other child in the class. This takes time but is a structured and relaxed way for children to begin forming relationships. Nancy loves how it helps the children get to know each other and also supports the idea that reading is a shared pleasure.

- Graphing the copyright dates. It's interesting to note that wonderful books can be of any vintage. Give this task to the fast worker who loves math.
- Taking a closer look at the authors. Have they written other books the students should know about?
- Having the children do a quick survey to find out how many others have read their favorite book.
- As the children talk about why a book is their favorite, using the information to start the reference chart "What Makes a Good Book."
- Having the children create personal reading time lines that shows highlights of their reading lives so far.

The length of time children spend with their favorite books depends on the class. Some years our exploration is rather brief and we move on to an author study within a few days. Other years the children's interest remains high and we continue our work with these books for a longer period of time. Whether three days or two weeks, asking children to bring in a favorite book is a worthwhile way to help children learn about each other as readers and classmates. It also sends the clear message: Children and books go together!

Creating Classroom Responsibilities

Responsibilities and expectations must be explicit and understood as the children move into their new school year together. I am continually grateful that the children I greet at the beginning of the year have come from fine classrooms where they have learned many important lessons about how to be a good group member. Nevertheless, it is crucial that we are all singing from the same song sheet. One of our first community building activities is to develop a list of what their responsibilities are to themselves and to the group. I used to make a list of class rules, but at a workshop with Kathy Doyle, an incredible teacher in Tenafly, New Jersey, she suggested replacing the word rules with responsibilities. It made sense. Rules can seem detached and imposed even if they are created by group consensus. Responsibilities imply active involvement and commitment.

I ask the children to write down five shared responsibilities that would keep our classroom a safe and beautiful place. Next I ask them to discuss their lists at a table of four. How do their lists compare? Next they are to choose the five responsibilities that are repeated on most lists. I collect and type up the five responsibilities suggested by each table. Later I pass them out to the class and we pare the list down to the most important ones. My aim is to have the list as succinct as possible. One responsibility on a long list can be ignored. On a shorter list, each responsibility grows in value.

This past fall, rather than asking students about their responsibilities, I asked them to list five ways they would like our class to be. Here are a few of their ideas:

- We help each other with kindness.
- We are responsible for our own things.
- We try to be peacemakers.

Then I asked the children at each table of four to choose one way they would like our class to be from our final list and to role-play a sixty-second scene to demonstrate what that would mean. My job was to videotape their skit after they had practiced. One stipulation was that everyone had to have an "on camera" part, even if it was just background. The whole process took several forty-five-minute work times and we were delighted with the results. The students enjoyed a chance to create their minidramas and learned more about each other as their group worked together. The video was strictly an amateur's production and took no more than six minutes of viewing time, but the process of cocreating was magical. Watching the final video, we felt like the winning team after the big game. The list of "Ways We Want Our Class to Be" now is on permanent display on the closet doors. To give it added importance and appeal, I photographed the class modeling each quality. The enlarged photos and words on laminated poster boards are a colorful confirmation of the best we can be.

Class Pattern

Doing knits the group together, and nothing can top the arts for inviting kids to *do*. The role-playing mentioned above and other activities in this chapter rely on the strength of the arts to connect children and give them a sense that they are of consequence in our classroom. Even something as simple as creating a class pattern has a powerful positive impact on their sense of belonging. Like the rhythmic drums around a fire brought ancient tribes together, on a much simpler scale, joining into a unified rhythm and pattern is another way for children to feel in sync with the group.

The first day of school I clapped and snapped a pattern and asked the children to repeat it (A B A-A B: clap snap clap-clap snap). We talked about an A-B pattern and I explained that the A would always be a clap but that the B part of the pattern would change. The second time the B part of the pattern was tapping my shoulders. The class watched and repeated the pattern. Next we put the two together. Then I asked what other movements we could use for the B part of the pattern. Elana suggested we drum on the tables. So we tried the three patterns in a row, first with the snap, then shoulder tap, then drum. I started a list under the title "Class Pattern." Each day the person of the day added another movement to the pattern. If they needed help with an idea, the class offered suggestions. Some of the movements suggested for the B part of the pattern were: elbow clap, cross and tap shoulders, fists (like in the hand-jive), wax it on (also from the hand-jive), angel clap (just clapping with index fingers), and thumbs (like two thumbs up for "Good job!"). Kids never fail to surprise me with their creative ideas. Part of the fun of the class pattern is giving each child a chance to add a movement. Younger children can do this kind of pattern and add new movements at a slower pace—perhaps once a week and return to the basic clap-snap pattern between each new movement. Older students may want to create a more complicated basic pattern.

Each time we do the class pattern I act as coach and call out the next movement. Of course, I am reading from the list on the bulletin board. This keeps us all together and creates an enthusiastic team spirit. Sometimes I'll use it as a refocus break or when we're waiting outside the music room because the teacher is running late. It's a lighthearted way to get the class with me that we both enjoy. It's also fun to show off for visitors who never fail to be impressed with our intricate-looking body choreography.

Swapping Summer Memories

After an active summer, the first few days of school the children need to be out of their seats and moving around the room with a purpose. I give them a class list, either with a box for each student or a line after the name. They also get their clipboard and a brief review of how they politely gather information from each other. Their job this time is to swap a summer memory with everyone in the class. When a child is asked for a memory, she may swap the same memory each time or she may use different ones. Children record a key word or two from each child as they move around the room filling in the information.

This is another opportunity for children to address their classmates, use their names, and find out something about each child. When the children finish, the follow-up activity depends on the age level and interest of the class and may develop from an idea or question posed by a student. The activity in the learning circle could be to ask, "Who would like to tell us one of Sharon's summer memories?" Children can take turns telling another child's memory. Again, children are hearing names in the group and learning how to be an active participant in the learning circle. Another activity is to categorize the memories and make a class graph.

Reference Charts

Creating reference charts together (see Chapter 3) is another key activity that continues throughout the year. Sharing their thinking and seeing the knowledge they construct together adds to the sense of community. In the first few weeks the class decides on responsibilities and may explore "What Makes a Good Book," "What We Can Write About Books," "What Good Readers Do as They Read," or "Story Ideas." Reference charts reinforce the central belief that everyone can contribute to the wealth of group information and knowledge. Asking children to draft their own list before they share as a group ensures that all children reflect on the topic and give it consideration.

Life Boxes

Life boxes are another surefire way to help kids get to know each other better. A life box is a collection of five objects stored in a small box, like a shoebox. I like to introduce life boxes by reading Mem Fox's unforgettable *Wilfred Gordon McDonald Partridge* (1985), a picture book about Wilfred Gordon, who helps Miss Nancy find her memory in a box of his treasured objects. Like Wilfred Gordon, "the small boy who wasn't very old either," I gather five objects that have a special meaning in my life. This year I included a playbill, because I love to go to the theatre. I also had a bookmark, a CD, a small cube that says "Writer's Block," and a picture of my family on Martha's Vineyard. I remove each object from my life box with reverence and tell the class a short anecdote about why it is important to me. Then children may ask me five questions. The first question is usually, "Can I bring in a life box?"

"Please do!" is my reply.

I send a note to parents asking them to monitor the contents of the box so precious family heirlooms stay at home and to help the children decide and limit their collection to five things that will be manageable on the school bus. The next morning counters begin to fill with odd-shaped boxes and lumpy bags. The children can barely wait to reveal their special things.

I schedule no more than three life box shares at a time and may do several sessions during the day. I want everyone to be a successful presenter and listener so I try to anticipate the number of life box shares the children can handle with interest. We sit in the learning circle and presenters display the contents of their life boxes. I am as fascinated as the children to know what everyone selected for their box. Among items shared one year were Danielle's bedroom slippers, because she loved to be cozy at home, Tyler's book about the presidents, because he loved to learn about them, and Michele's baby blanket her grandma had made for her.

Sharing a life box provides a spotlight for each child. The children discover new facets of their classmates and have an opportunity to reflect on what is significant in their own lives. When everyone has had an opportunity to share their life box—and this may take up to a week or longer—we sit in the learning circle and reminisce. What object do they especially remember from a life box? What did they learn about someone that may have surprised them? Why was it important to take the time to share life boxes? I also talk about how life boxes are a treasure trove of writing ideas.

ACTIVITIES THAT NOURISH
AND STRENGTHEN RELATIONSHIPS
THROUGHOUT THE YEAR

Class Meetings

Problem solving together is an important ingredient in a classroom of healthy peer relationships. Regularly scheduled class meetings provide the time and opportunity for children to address issues that are of concern to them. The format of the meetings needs to be set and practiced so children know the emphasis is on solving problems and not complaining. Courtesy helps protect children from emotions that can escalate.

There are many ways to organize class meetings. I like to start and end mine with a ritual. We begin by "saying in" acts of kindness we have noticed since the last meeting. Children learn these must be honest observations and not just a way to stroke the ego of a friend. The agenda is set and announced in advance so the children have time to consider their opinion about the topic. They may offer suggestions for the agenda by signing up on the bulletin board. The agenda is short and the meeting is limited to fifteen minutes. The meeting ends with a group poem or chant, something that builds a sense of team.

Small-Group Activities

"Small group collaboration works," write Harvey Daniels and Marilyn Bizar in *Methods That Matter: Six Structures for Best Practice Classrooms* (1998). Partnerships and small groups allow children to fully participate in conversations as they grapple with topics and problems worth thinking about. When children think out loud with each other, their relationship to the material and to each other deepens. With definite guidelines for working effectively with a partner, small group activities give a needed energy boost to young learners.

Last Friday the children numbered off to play a math game with a partner. The duets dispersed around the room and I watched and listened as they took turns throwing the dice and recording their score. The room was filled with cooperation and commitment to the task. At the end of math time we met in our learning circle and I told the class what I had noticed. "You just did it so well," I remarked. "Let's make a list of 'What Makes a Good Partner.' Describe what made your partnership work." Here's the list they developed:

A GOOD PARTNER

1. doesn't brag
2. isn't bossy
3. is a good sport
4. listens to you
5. doesn't fool around

The reference chart reflects the qualities important to the students and, I imagine, to most individuals in a partnership. We will revisit the list the next time we form partnerships. The list has more weight because it was drafted fresh from a successful partnership. If the assigned activity matches their interest and developmental level and I have given clear directions, there is a greater likelihood of success. Misunderstandings in small groups are often the result of confusion about what to do.

I no longer make the assumption that children inherently have the social skills necessary to make a good partner or small group member. Therefore, early in the year I limit the groups to partnerships or no more than three children since the larger the group the more demands it places on the social skills of the members. I want to ensure the success of independent pairs and trios before dividing them into larger groups. These may evolve as we work our way into reading clubs and small writing response groups.

Children need choices in their school day and I used to struggle with the issue of assigning partners when I asked them to work on a cooperative project. Would they work better with a partner of their choice? Once I made the decision to assign random partners for some of their work, I discovered the advantages usually outweigh their desire to make the choice.

When children choose their own partners or groups, there is always the moment when the unchosen straggle over with that look of rejection. "I don't have a partner," they announce. "No one wants to work with me." Some quick problem solving and shuffling usually resolves the grouping, but it is never easy to watch the same children be left out of the social musical chairs.

Often best friends turn out to be worst partners. Or if friends are struggling with a problem, the added strain of a working partnership, deciding who calls the shots, and so on, can tip the balance of the relationship into negativity. A clean slate often seems to serve the class better. Of course, we spend time before we work with partners talking about what it means to be a good partner. Children know what it takes to be a cooperative group member even if they can't always do it. Setting the guidelines helps them to know what to expect as they get to work.

As we sit in the learning circle, I have the children number off to twelve. The ones work together, and the twos, and so on. I joke with them that this partnership is just for the next half hour or maybe a few days if there is a more involved project to do. It's not a date or marriage. Oddly enough, the fates usually provide partnerships that make it. As the children spread out around the room to work together on the assigned task, I marvel at their willingness to give cooperation a try. With clear expectations that everyone in the class can and will work together, they rise to the high standard.

Work time ends with a quick reflection and evaluation:

> Please rate with your fingers how well you worked with your partner. A "4" means you did your best to get along and were able to compromise. A "3" means you were able to work pretty well together. A "2" means you had trouble reaching agreements, but still kept going.

I don't ask about a "1" rating because I would have intervened if a partnership were having serious problems. Sometimes I may ask them to rate how they felt about the working partnership, but only if I know ahead of time from the sense of the group that they are feeling successful and positive. If groups did not go well, we will focus on what they could do differently next time. The success of the group ultimately rests with me and how succinctly I gave the directions. Partners that are unsure of the task can spend their time arguing over what they're supposed to do. Clear directions and expectations provide a solid foundation for these temporary teams. From them, new relationships can be formed that help to strengthen the social fabric of the class. When Charles worked with Zach to read and find interesting facts, the two boys beamed with their sense of accomplishment. They might not choose to play together at recess, but they gained a respect for each other as they read and worked together. They made each other feel of consequence. Their work was better because of their combined efforts.

When children are assigned random partners, I try to build in choices in other ways. For instance, they can choose whether to sit at their tables, on the small stools, or on the floor. Within the parameters of the task I also try to build in a choice—students may decide to read quietly to each other or silently. This may necessitate the pair reaching a compromise, but that is a skill worth the practice.

While the children are busy in their partnerships, I circulate and confer with groups, especially ones that may initially need extra support to get started. There are some days when the assignment does not get done with the same flourish that I may have hoped for from all the groups, but the social interactions sparkled with careful listening and kindness. In the long run, I know we came out victorious.

Working with a partner or in a small group is part of daily life in my classroom. If I assign random partners for one assignment, I try to balance it with other opportunities for children to choose their own partners at another time. What I observe as the children work together gives me information about our social climate and helps me to decide how to group them next time.

Celebrating Birthdays

People who care about each other celebrate birthdays in ceremonial and fun ways. I want the birthday routine to seem special, but not to be so cumbersome that I abandon it after the tenth one we celebrate. I don't want to mimic the family pattern of elaborate and extensive photo albums for the first child and a few miscellaneous pictures of the third. I have to be sure that the June and summer birthdays feel as welcome as the September celebrations. Following are some of the ways I have found to keep birthdays joyful and practical.

Party Place Mats. Sometime during the first few weeks of school when the children seem to need a quiet art project, I get out twelve-by-eighteen-inch white construction paper and the markers we use for special projects and best work. The students create a colorful and festive party place mat that includes their name. The place mat will be used for each birthday and holiday celebration, so I encourage them to make a place mat that will help them feel good each time it's used. We brainstorm a few ideas and they set to work.

Once the students finish their drawings and designs, I have them laminated. The plastic coating allows spilled punch and cupcake crumbs to wipe right off and it's easier for the children to shake a place mat over the wastebasket than it is to get sticky crumbs off the table tops.

Party place mats set the stage for each small but significant celebration. As the birthday child passes out the party place mats, the children clear their space in anticipation. Like putting the tablecloth on the dining room table for company, the party place mats signal that the celebration is about to begin.

Birthday Wishes. The morning of the birthday, class members make a sheet much like a reading response sheet. There is a space for a picture and four or five lines for a message. Across the top in a fancy font it says "Birthday Wishes." Each child writes a birthday wish and draws a colorful illustration for the birthday child.

We spend time talking about how the birthday wish should be specific, although, depending on the grade level, even more generic wishes bring smiles of gratitude from the receiver. While the rest of the class is working on their birthday wish, the birthday child decorates the cover for the birthday wishes booklet on white oak tag paper. As the children finish their wishes, they hang them on the chalkboard beneath a "Happy Birthday" greeting with the child's name. The cheerful wishes and colorful drawings lend a note of festivity. The next day, when the wishes from each child are done, I spiral-bind the wishes into a birthday book. When I first did birthday wishes, I tried to get them bound and ready on the birthday, but that caused too much pressure and sapped some of the joy for me and the children who like to take their time. The birthday wishes booklet is a delightful gift to receive even a few days after the birthday.

To help keep the quality of the birthday wishes high, we create a reference chart for what makes a "4" birthday wish. A list from one second-grade class said:

A "4" BIRTHDAY WISH HAS

1. colorful illustration
2. careful printing
3. correct spelling
4. a special wish for that child
5. your name on the paper
6. your best work

Hanging the wishes on the chalkboard for others to see also encourages children to take pride in their work.

Party Manners. The children I teach come from homes where manners are taught and practiced. Nevertheless, a party atmosphere can sometimes bring out their worst eating habits as children vie to entertain each other with food stunts. So before our first birthday celebration we make a reference chart of party manners. (Yes, we do other things besides reference charts, but they save so much time in the long run!) I want my expectations perfectly clear as the kids enjoy cupcakes and juice together. A quick reference to these before subsequent birthdays underscores their importance.

The Celebration. Our birthday celebration is brief, and yet it seems to satisfy the children. First the birthday child and several selected friends pass out the party place mats and birthday treats. Then the child (and parents if they choose to be there) sits on a special stool as the class sings "Happy Birthday"—the updated version with "cha-cha-cha" inserted after each line of the song. I've heard several fun birthday songs; some classes have sung more than one song or the birthday child chooses which song the class sings. The children wait until the birthday child has had the first bite of cupcake or drink of juice and then everyone enjoys the sweet break in the routine. Probably the most exciting part of the celebration is choosing a friend or two and taking a cupcake to the principal's office. I think that walk down the hall with a cupcake is one of the proudest moments for many young celebrants.

Kindergarten Partners

Mentoring younger students brings out the best in children. A favorite time for me is when my third graders meet with their kindergarten partners for a thirty-five minute writing workshop. Bobbi Hauer—an energetic, creative, and highly organized kindergarten teacher—and I meet briefly in September to match up our children. Which of my children could handle a boisterous kindergartener? Which third grader would encourage a shy child? We play our hunches and are most often delighted with the way the pairs work together. We schedule our meetings for every other week, set the date of the first encounter, and we're on our way.

This year, Bobbi suggested we meet the first time in my room and that the older children read aloud to their younger partners. Partner reading proved to be a relaxed and comfortable way for the children to get acquainted. Two weeks later we met in the kindergarten room. Bobbi explained to my students how to help their younger partners with their writing. Within five minutes, twenty-three pairs of children were scattered throughout the room chatting in quiet voices, heads bent over drawings of cats, superheroes, and rainbows. Bobbi and I looked at each other over the roomful of engrossed children. This was exactly what we had hoped for!

For the rest of the year, we divided the classes in half. One time I would have Group A and the next time Group B. The kindergarten children continued to work on their stories and the third graders took pride in the progress of the younger writers. Last year, we also scheduled two poetry sessions where we recited favorite poems for each other. Third graders also helped their partners with nonfiction research in the school library. Heads bent over books about bears, they walked through the pictures and gathered facts. Another time Bobbi suggested we give the children a choice time. She'd noticed how the third graders were eyeing the many attractive kindergarten activities in her room. Partners in both rooms built with blocks or Legos, played card games, painted pictures, and found other relaxing ways to share their time. Popcorn added to the sense of joyful togetherness.

When we meet with our kindergarten partners, the third graders demand more of themselves. Their whole demeanor changes. Suddenly they are the older, more experienced, more knowledgeable exemplar of proper school behavior. They walk taller, listen with more patience, speak with more thoughtfulness. Classmates see each other in this more mature and responsible role. For a brief and shining moment they have increased their stature with their peers because of their caring attitude toward a younger child. In a most perfect world, all students would interact the way these caring older children do with their young partners. It doesn't get any better.

If you don't already have such a partnership with another teacher, try to make arrangements. It doesn't take much coordination after the initial meeting to pair up the students and the rewards for the students and the teacher are immeasurable.

Super Clean

Super Clean is a way to get the class working like a team to make the classroom sparkle. It is a highly visible indicator that a team effort really makes a difference. Everyone is included in cleaning the room. Our custodians vacuum our rooms, but can't be expected to dust bookcases, scrub countertops, or clean the dust that accumulates between the computers. Children love to clean, as long as they are shown how and it's not their bedroom.

First I divide the room into twelve specific cleaning jobs (since I have twenty-four children in my class) such as washing the chalkboard, scrubbing tabletops, washing chair seats, dusting bookshelves. I list the twelve jobs on chart paper and give a quick overview of each job. Next, the children number off so that everyone has a partner. Each partnership is assigned to a specific task. For example, Michael and Marisa are to take everything off the windowsill, dust it, and wash it. Max and Diane are to organize the books on the black bookcase and clean the shelves. Zach and C. J. are to clear everything off the back counter, scrub it, and put everything back neatly. Kristina and Paige are assigned to carefully clean the computer screens.

When Max and Diane were having a difficult time working together, it was easier to negotiate a solution around the physical task of cleaning than an academic or personal issue. They were able to complete their task and showed a noticeable pride in the fact that they had worked through their conflict *and* that the black bookcase looked brand-new. The next Super Clean they asked to work together again.

What's amazing about Super Clean is the way the kids pitch in and work. A roll of better-grade paper towel, a squirt bottle of an environmentally safe cleaner, and the students become an energetic cleaning machine. I walk around passing out paper towels and spritzing surfaces when requested. The students do the rest. They feel a sense of accomplishment when their paper towel gets grubby with accumulated grime. "Look at how dirty this was, Mrs. Skolnick!" Paige exclaimed in mock horror.

Scubbing away dust and dirt gives kids a sense of satisfaction and the room takes on a new shine. Assigning areas and partners has worked well for me. About once a month or when company is coming, the class goes into high gear to Super Clean. The completed job is accompanied by statements like, "The room has never been so clean!" and "We have the cleanest room in the building!" And we do! Their sense of camaraderie and achievement puts a sparkle on their faces as well as the room.

IT IS IMPERATIVE THAT CHILDREN MAKE CONNECTIONS TO EACH other in the classroom. These relationships nourish the learning environment in ways that we did not understand when I was a child in school. In *Emotional Intelligence*, Daniel Goleman writes

> We transmit and catch moods from each other in what amounts to a sub-terranean economy of the psyche in which some encounters are toxic, some are nourishing. This emotional exchange is typically at a subtle, almost im-perceptible level; . . . we catch feelings from one another as though they were some kind of social virus. (114)

As the teachers in charge, we have the power to ensure vigorous con-nections or to short-circuit social skills. Children sitting in rows restricted to peer interactions at lunch or on the playground find school a lonely place. Like the little boy who took only a postage-size piece of his special blanket to school when he started kindergarten, children not connected to their class-mates bring only a small piece of themselves to school each day. Their spe-cialness remains concealed.

Whether kids perceive themselves inside or outside a group has direct bearing on their attitude, behavior, and ability to learn. Teachers create and support caring relationships among students as they provide time and rou-tines for relationships to flourish. Helping all children have a strong sense of membership in the classroom can initially feel as insurmountable as compos-ing a symphony. Yet when the connectedness happens, it is one of those ordi-nary miracles that makes teaching the best profession in the world.

6

The Relationship Between the Teacher and the Curriculum

Reading and writing curriculum at the elementary level share a broad common objective: by the time kids move on to middle school with its oozing pubescence, they efficiently use reading and writing as tools for learning. Like driving from New York City to Los Angeles, there are as many routes to this curriculum destination as there are travelers. What impacts the journey more than the route mapped out by curriculum guides (which are often determined by publishers) is the teacher's personal relationship to literacy. She can see reading and writing as mandated subjects to teach or as central to who she is. Her concern could be that children read and write well enough to pass the next standardized test or whether students care as much as she does about reading, writing, and learning.

Regardless of the curriculum in place in our schools, it is our own belief in the transformational power of reading and writing that carries the day. In order for children to aspire to be accomplished readers and writers, they must spend their days with teachers who are an inspiration. For some children, learning to read seems as natural as learning to laugh. For others, it's more like learning to swim in the cold Atlantic with a strong undertow and jellyfish. If learning to swim promises future calm, azure blue waters with colorful coral reefs for snorkeling, the toil and fear of learning lessens. That's where a passionate, joyfully literate teacher comes in. She'll search to discover the appropriate skill or strategy to teach next, to find the just-right books, and she's there to applaud the progress. Reading specialist, librarian, and cheerleader rolled into one, she's tenacious about all children learning to love books and language. Unless the teachers draws on her personal love of literacy to sustain her efforts and convince children of their merits, only the natural readers will establish their own indefatigable connections to reading and writing.

When I was in first grade I wanted to be just like my teacher, Mrs. Howe, with her tight bun and perfect printing. I want the children in my class to wish to grow up to be like their teacher: someone who loves to read and write. My own habits as a reader and writer play a powerful role in the learning exchange. If I present the curriculum without real zest and joy, it doesn't matter what methods, materials, or mandated curriculum I use. The students are not going to buy it.

As a teacher fresh from the college campus, the curriculum was handed to me. I handed it on to students as something they were simply expected to do, like sit quietly in their seats. It was a one-size-fits-all curriculum. If some children didn't learn as quickly, perhaps they weren't trying hard enough, paying close enough attention.

As time passed and my dissatisfaction with the teaching-equals-learning equation grew, I tried other ways to organize my classroom so all children could meet success. The open classroom movement in the early seventies taught me how to structure my classroom for more of a flow. It invited student choice and independence. I set up centers, wrote learning task cards, and the classroom was starting to feel more aligned with the needs and styles of children. Then the back to basics backlash dropped a wet blanket on the open classroom fires of excitement. Work jobs and hands-on materials were shoved into the closet to be replaced by an easier way to teach—basals and workbooks. The only problem was, it was a harder way for many children to learn.

Dedicated teachers continued to search for a better way to help children as readers and writers. Low and behold! Answers began to emerge—not from on high, not from curriculum pundits or publishers, but at the grassroots level, one fine teacher at a time, exploring and inventing ways that worked for kids. Don Graves, Lucy Calkins, and Susan Sowers moved in with Mary Ellen Giocobbe's first graders at Atkinson Academy in Atkinson, New Hampshire, for two years to research their habits and growth as writers. Graves's book *Writing: Teachers and Children at Work* (1983) awakened teachers to a writing potential in young children they had never imagined. Nancie Atwell shared her remarkable classroom research in *In the Middle* (1998), and Lucy McCormick Calkins's book *The Art of Teaching Writing* (1994) captured teachers' attention with its sensitive stories of young writers and sage advice for helping them grow.

Close on the heels of these new discoveries about the power of the workshop setting and untapped student potential followed the whole language movement. Focus shifted from reading programs that taught prescribed skills in a sequence for all children to a more holistic approach to literacy. The whole language movement challenged traditional beliefs about how children learn to read and write and a polemic developed. Research continues as we try to understand how children learn. Brain-based research contributes additional information to our growing body of knowledge.

Gerald Duffy and James Hoffman, in their 1999 article "In Pursuit of an Illusion: The Flawed Search for a Perfect Method," state:

> Of much greater importance is our responsibility for replacing the perfect method concept with a commitment to developing independent, problem-solving, and spirited teachers who understand that their job is to use many good methods and materials in various ways according to students' needs. (15)

The jewel in the crown, the icing on the cake, the air conditioning in the classroom is the teacher who has a variety of teaching strategies, who demonstrates that reading is great fun—a forever pleasure and resource, and worthy of students' best efforts.

My own joyful literacy forges my connection to the curriculum. First and foremost I want students to see me as someone who loves to learn, to read, to write, as someone who has hundreds of favorite books, who delights in ideas and the language of fine stories, who wonders about the world and all its mysteries. I want children to know that my relationship to reading and writing is alive and energized. My habits of mind stimulate my thinking about books, about my writing, about my life. I am passionate about the written word for myself and for students. The work we do each day in reading and writing rests solidly on my own resilient relationship to those subjects.

Katherine Paterson says it so well in *The Spying Heart* (1989): "Perhaps this is the way to teach children. First, we must love music or literature or mathematics or history or science so much that we cannot stand to keep that love to ourselves. Then with the energy and enthusiasm and enormous respect for the learner, we share our love" (142).

My authority in the classroom comes from my love of reading and writing, not a curriculum guide. It is my deep abiding passion for language and story that radiates out and nudges the desire in the children to be readers and writers, too. I don't have to tell them that I love books; they see it, they feel it. And they want in on that satisfying secret. Readers and writers possess a certain magic that allows them to transform through words—a magic that is enticing and captivating. What a rare gift of wonder to offer to students each day. Literacy is a glittering treasury full of stories, charms, and secrets: words that whisper and words that roar; words that bring chills and words that bring smiles; words that change lives and words that connect child to story, child to child, and child to teacher.

BEING A READER AND A WRITER

Of course, teachers teach, but finding ways to read and write with the children on a regular basis deepens the teacher's relationship to reading and writing. No longer an inherited manual with prescribed lessons, reading becomes a human endeavor shared by those who are learning and growing. When the teacher reads and writes with the class, it is like yeast to bread dough. All are elevated.

At a recent workshop teachers were talking about the importance of writing in front of the children and sharing our writing with them. One teacher asked, "Would it be the end of the world if I didn't write with the class?" Before I could formulate a diplomatic answer, I blurted, "Yes!" I hadn't realized until that question how strongly I felt. The teacher as both reader and writer impacts the classroom dynamic in indelible ways. Later that evening, I remembered this incident from my childhood, triggered by that question:

> The summer when I was nine my mother decided to enroll me in a swimming class where I would learn to dive. On the morning of memory the smiling instructor showed us how to position our feet, arms, and torso over the chilly lake before the graceful plunge into its murky depths. Time after time I gripped the edge of the board with my toes, formed a V with my arms, and entered the water with the full impact of a large rubber pancake. Splat! Repeatedly I dragged my reddened and shivering body up the wooden ladder to be reminded how to do it properly. It was simple. I just had to be sure to tuck my chin. Splat again! As my body and ego grew increasingly battered, I became more and more annoyed that my smiling instructor had not even been in the cold lake. Her bathing suit was still dry! I didn't even know if she *could* dive. She only told me what to do.

I used that young instructor as a scapegoat for my own sense of failure. I just would have felt better, more supported, if she had dived into the water, too. Her dry bathing suit is a metaphor for how some young learners feel in school. Writing can feel like diving into the frightening depths and when the repeated attempts are belly flops, the diving board gets higher and the lake colder. Putting pencil to paper can be terrifying and uncomfortable. When the teacher never uncaps her pen except to circle errors, it somehow seems even more daunting.

Ideally all schools would be like The Manhattan New School in New York City where the scholarly lives of teachers are a top priority. In *Going Public* (1999), then MNS principal Shelley Harwayne describes the many ways the school community supports the literacy of the adults in the building. She quotes Rexford Brown: "Anyone who hopes to excite and challenge young people without exciting and challenging their teachers hopes in vain" (241).

PERSONAL MEANING IN THE CURRICULUM

I assume responsibility for making the curriculum enhance the language arts abilities of all the children in my class regardless of their ability level or personality or learning style. As I learn about their literacy development, I am able to play matchmaker and mentor. But for all this to be possible, I must find my own personal meaning in what the curriculum offers. Unless I connect to the curriculum at a personal and meaningful level, I will be unable to help students make that connection.

It is more difficult to establish a salient relationship with the curriculum when it feels a mile wide and an inch deep. I heard Howard Gardner speak at the 42nd Street Library in New York City last year. One piece of advice stood out regarding curriculum. He asks teachers to pretend they have but one hour to teach all they would hope to teach in a year. What is it that they would choose to emphasize in that hour? Teach *that* every day.

After hearing Dr. Gardner, I realized the following five qualities are my one hour of curriculum. I teach these five concepts each and every hour of reading in infinite ways.

1. *Readers choose to read.* I help students discover the magic of reading, how it transcends place and time. Reading is not a school assignment.
2. *Readers know how to choose books.* I give students strategies and opportunities for finding books they enjoy and want to read. When the book is the wrong fit, reading feels like a chore.
3. *Readers understand and remember what they read.* I help students learn skills and strategies so they can be fluent, comprehending readers.
4. *Readers read for a variety of purposes.* I help students know the many ways books, magazines, and other forms of writing, make our lives better.
5. *Readers talk with other readers.* I give students the structures and time to learn the satisfaction of talking with other readers, either for recommendations or to exchange questions and ideas.

This list easily transforms to fit the writing curriculum. The five qualities I want the writers in my class to have are:

1. *Writers choose to write.* I help students to gain the confidence and competency to view writing as an important tool in their lives.
2. *Writers know how to choose topics and audience.* I give students many opportunities to think like a writer and make the decisions writers make.
3. *Writers write to make meaning and to communicate.* I support students with strategies and crafting lessons as they learn to match their intentions to their writing.
4. *Writers write for a variety of purposes.* I help students see the many ways writing is used in the school setting and in their lives.
5. *Writers talk with other writers.* I give students structures and time to talk with classmates and other writers about their ideas and processes.

These are ambitious lists but they keep me focused on what contributes most to the literary life of young readers and writers. My goal is to instill these ten qualities of what proficient readers and writers do. When I model what they mean in my life, there is a value added.

There are other qualities, attitudes, and intentions that influence my relationship to and delivery of the reading/writing curriculum. If I am passionate about reading, but overzealous in my interactions with children, my extreme enthusiasm may seem like I'm overly anxious to sell them shoddy goods. The rest of this chapter is dedicated to my list of other key factors that affect how I present reading and writing to students.

1. THE WHY, WHAT, HOW, AND WHO OF MY TEACHING

Since I first started teaching three decades ago, the *why* I teach has not changed. I want to share my own love of language and learning with children and help them to become joyfully literate. I also make my *why* explicit to the children. I explain why what we do will help them become better readers and writers.

My *what* and *how* have changed dramatically. Gone are the three reading groups patiently plodding through a basal reader and workbook. Gone is my lack of faith in a book and a child to find each other. In this golden age of children's literature, my classroom is now crammed with reading choices. My role has changed from managing a reading program to matching and connecting children with books and helping them develop the skills and strategies to understand and enjoy what they read and write.

A workshop format for reading and writing times invites all learners to be insiders in the literacy club. It changes the flavor of the room from vanilla to many delicious options. The simple design of minilesson, independent work time, and group share provides the organization, structure, and flexibility for diverse learning to unfold.

Workshops offer a broader canvas for the reading and writing classroom. Sometimes I feel like we give students a postage stamp on which to think and work. I want children to feel like they have a canvas the size of the gym floor where they can do their finest work. Such a setting permits students to establish an individual and resilient relationship to reading and writing—the deciding factor in how children view their literacy.

My *who,* my inner landscape, has also changed. The self who teaches is more aware, more authentic, more compassionate, most of the time. As Parker J. Palmer writes in *The Courage to Teach* (1998), "Teaching, like any human activity, emerges from one's inwardness, for better or worse. As I teach, I project the condition of my soul onto my students, my subject, and our way of being together" (2). Psychologists and educators acknowledge the role of the teacher's inner life, a topic unconsidered in traditional conversations about school. In many ways, the *who* we are as teachers is an unacknowledged curriculum. Our values and beliefs come through our every action in subtle and unexpected ways. How we perceive the curriculum and our relationship to it cannot be filtered out of our daily school lives. Even children who cannot read can read between the lines.

2. EMBRACING THE UNKNOWN

Last November at the NCTE convention in Nashville, I happened to go to a workshop entitled "Finding the Energy, Renewing the Spirit," presented by Dr. Daniel Lindley of the Chicago Jungian Institute. I was in the right place at the right time. For ninety minutes I frantically took notes. Dr. Lindley was giving this workshop for me. Judging by the energy in the room and the rapt attention, the rest of the audience felt the same way. What he said made sense, and yet how could I have taught since Lyndon Johnson was President and not have known what Dr. Lindley was saying? He was answering so many of my own deep questions about classroom teaching.

What I hadn't considered until that moment of *eureka!* were the unexplored reasons I had chosen teaching as a profession in the first place. Most people assume teachers are founts of knowledge about a favorite subject and want to pass along that learning. But that's only a fraction of it. Teachers love the unknown, Dr. Lindley explained. It is the *not* knowing that awakens us, not the volumes on our bookshelves that we already know. Our childlike quest for learning propelled many of us into teaching. It is what we don't know that fascinates us. When the curious child in us recedes, when the excitement of the unknown dissipates, then our energy wanes and we are disconnected from our source of inspiration. Healthy teaching means the seeking inner child is alive and well.

"Not knowing, that is, being willing to admit that we don't know, is one of the keys that opens the door to creative intelligence," write Richard Carlson and Joseph Bailey in *Slowing Down to the Speed of Life* (1997, 21). Perhaps that is one reason why not knowing can feel positive and energizing. We are open to new ideas and solutions.

3. THE ABILITY TO BE PLAYFUL

As I heard Dr. Lindley speak, a new definition of Vivian Paley's book *You Can't Say You Can't Play* flitted across my mind. Teachers, too, should not be allowed to proclaim, "I don't play in my classroom." Teachers who are so serious and set against lighthearted enjoyment of children and learning may need to seek other means of financial support. Those of us who spend our days among children must be able to *play* in the highest sense of the word. In the loving and joyful attention we give to the students, in our pleasure in their company, in our spirited search for new understandings of them and how they learn, in all these and numerous other ways we keep our own inner child thriving. When we've been there, done that, when there's nothing new to write on the chalkboard, then it's time to dust the chalk off our hands and move along.

It is our own questioning inner child who reaches out and connects with students. It's what allows me to look at Matthew and see the same overeager attention-seeker I was in second grade. Or when Jackie fumbles with a new piece of writing, I see my own uncertainty writing report cards. Or when Alexandra reads her part in the play with a perfect British accent, I remember that proud moment from my own young performances. We connect heart to heart.

I need to go back to the word *play* for just a minute. I'm not referring to a child's definition of play that means you do whatever you want whenever you want to do it. My definition of *play* is an attitude, an acceptance of *what is* that allows me to find a richness in each moment. It's adding grace to the grit of daily life. It's seeing the humor in small things and taking the time to appreciate. Play lightens the load while it increases the output. It's what I don't do

well when my head is stuffy or when my mind is wandering. I know I'm feeling better when I sing a reminder song to clean up, rather than giving worn-
out verbal reminders. It's like the difference between lunch at a favorite French
restaurant with red-checkered tablecloths and lunch in the school cafeteria
with peanut butter stuck to the table. Both meals nourish; one nourishes the
spirit as well. I can't always choose where I want to eat, but I can choose to take
a sense of play with me into the classroom. Regardless of the grade I teach or
the subject I'm teaching, my ability to be playful, especially with a large group
of children, is one I work to improve.

4. THE SOURCE OF GOOD TEACHING

In *This Rough Magic: The Life of Teaching*, Dr. Lindley asserts that there are
two kinds of teaching: "Teaching driven by the will and teaching driven by
imagination. Although they often overlap in real classrooms, they may be
separated for the purpose of analysis and reflection" (1993, 45). His differen-
tiation hinges on how the teacher perceives students. When she sees herself in
the position of power over students, the source of her teaching is will. In this
power position, students become those without power. When the teacher
imagines competence and knowing in her students, a different kind of energy
exchange takes place and they are energized by their felt sense of connection.
"The recognition of such equality by the teacher is the moral center of teaching. It is the place where neither power or subservience operates" (49).

I have greatly simplified the exciting information in Dr. Lindley's book,
but this underlying premise adds another critical layer of awareness about the
complexities of classroom teaching and learning. When the teacher relates to
the curriculum as a body of knowledge that she *will* teach through her own
determination and domination, that relationship is rigid and fragile. Teaching
by imagination envisions possibilities. The mind is open and creatively alert.
Opportunities for connectedness abound and the relationship between the
teacher and the curriculum blossoms.

5. TREAT THEM LIKE THEY KNOW

"Treat them [students] like they know." These words flew by me in a conversation and I snatched them out of the air. They reinforce my belief system about how to interact with children. When I talk to them as if they already possess an understanding and wisdom that resides deep within, I
activate their inner knowing-adult. I listen for their knowing, rather than their
not-knowing. As we create reference charts together, as we discuss what we
know about books, or how to treat others with kindness, my appreciation for

what they contribute triggers their latent knowledge. We amaze ourselves with insights and understandings. If I had not asked for their thoughts, we may never have known their possibilities. Reference charts and group discussions make their knowing conscious and explicit.

Once a former principal observed how I managed a reading group. The children and I sat in a circle on the rug as we discussed a short book. Later in our postconference, the principal commented, "You seemed so interested in their answers to your questions." I wasn't just a good actress. I *was* interested in what each child was thinking. Hearing their unexpected thoughts can be the best part of the day. I love having wonderful ideas as I'm teaching. It's even more exciting when children have the wonderful ideas. My job is to tap into these ideas and bring them to the foreground.

6. TEACHER AS RESEARCHER

Being part of a formal Teacher as Researcher program at Teachers College with Lucy Calkins in the 1980s was a pivotal point in my teaching and my relationship to the curriculum. Our group of six writing staff developers from different suburban school districts met with Lucy each Thursday afternoon. She pushed and pulled our thinking and gave us the courage to do the same back in our districts. For two years I ran a teacher as researcher group with ten colleagues. We posed our own questions and then used our classrooms as our primary source of information. When Mary Lou Woodruff wanted to know what helped her third graders most as a writer, she asked them. "Group share!" was their resounding response. As we began to listen closely to the wisdom of our students, our excitement grew. We had tapped into the mother lode. Why hadn't we realized before that we could ask children? Maybe we hadn't had the courage. Then again, why bother asking children what makes a difference for them unless we were willing to make changes?

Writing workshop and teacher as researcher rewrote the daily classroom script for me. Imitating an assignment Nancie Atwell had given at a summer workshop, I asked a class of fifth-grade students to write "I am a writer because . . . " or "I am not a writer because. . . ." The previous school year I had worked in their fourth-grade classrooms as they wrote stories from prompts with our former writing program. My job had been to meet with them and correct what they had written before they recopied it in final form. Of course, I had many helpful revisions.

I had been clueless about all my advice. One fifth grader wrote: "I am not a writer. The teacher changes everything I write." Another child wrote, "I am not a writer, I am a finisher. I write just to get the assignment done."

I read their responses and knew there was a way I could help them as writers. Over the summer I had learned about writing workshop from Nancie

Atwell, Mary Ellen Giocobbe, and Don Graves. With the help of my colleagues, I could change the writing curriculum. I could give students choices about topic, about revisions, about how long to work on a piece. I could invite them to share their work with classmates and not be the sole reader and judge. And I could keep asking questions.

Turning to children and asking "Is this working?" threw open the windows to more enchanting options and shifted the balance in the classroom. As the senior learner, I could continue my personal quest to grow as a teacher while helping students improve the quality of their learning.

This same discovery—that the voices of children enhance what we do in the name of learning—led to constructing knowledge together and writing reference charts. "What do you think?" became a serious and earnest question.

My relationship to the curriculum changed. I was no longer the guardian of the gates of knowledge, doling out small parcels of precious information from the district scope and sequence. Instead, adding the children as a legitimate resource, I discovered I could enrich the classroom learning, making it more relevant and applicable. Erik Erikson in *Identity and the Life Cycle* (1964) gives still another reason why turning to the students for their ideas is valuable: We need their insights and energy to help renew our own lives. When we view our students as incredibly rich resources waiting and hoping to be mined, classroom learning becomes heartier and more nutritious.

7. CONVERSATIONS THAT SUPPORT OUR WORK

Membership in a teacher as researcher group contributed insight and energy to my teaching. Teachers at Kings Highway Elementary School in Westport have found a way to strengthen teachers' relationship to the curriculum and each other as they talk and write informally about their classrooms. Seven years ago Dr. Karen Ernst daSilva began a Community of Teachers Learning, known as COTL. Teachers meet every other week to write a brief reflection and talk about classroom issues. COTL is a safe and supportive place to share successes, frustrations, and even failures. Kings Highway is a school with open doors, open minds, and open hearts. The trusting connections among the staff spill over into the classrooms and set the school tone of learning and sharing together. They have discovered a way to deisolate teaching.

Having come to teaching when doors were closed and collegial conversations were surface courtesies, the contrast feels bold. How refreshing to know the teachers at other grade levels as professional colleagues who share similar hopes and concerns. How reassuring to hear the stories of the teacher down the hall and know that we are on the same wavelength. When the absorbing work we do is nourished and supported by conversations with colleagues, it eases the sense of separateness so often experienced in the school setting. And it's helpful to know that we're not the only one who would like to push the rewind button and start some days over. Laughter and tears shared with those dedicated to the same mission feels like curling up with a favorite old quilt.

Heartfelt conversations with colleagues about our teaching help create new connections of meaning to the curriculum. As we share book titles, nonfiction ideas, the words of our students that have made us laugh with pleasure, or other thoughts, we learn new perspectives and possibilities. Teachers on grade-level teams who collaborate and plan together display more energy and enthusiasm than teachers who tend to go it alone. The camaraderie of colleagues who work just as hard, care just as much, invent just as creatively infuses life at school with a special glow.

8. TIME TO REFLECT

Reflection never used to be a priority for me as a teacher. The demands of school and family squeezed out a regular time to think in-depth about how things were going. The drive to and from school provided my time for a few quiet thoughts. Otherwise, like the express train that doesn't stop in a smaller town, my thoughts whizzed on by. Then I discovered the power of reflecting for a few minutes on paper. The act of writing about my day or week opened up another channel of awareness. My journal entries gave me unexpected insights into what I was doing and how it was working. Slowing down to write gave my inner voice a chance to be heard. My intuitive self, who may get ignored in the rush of the day, was able to step forth onto the paper and generate ideas and understandings. By taking time to reflect, I gave myself the gift of mindfulness and a way to witness my own growth over time.

The most powerful reflections were those done with other committed colleagues. Thinking and writing together leads to the rich and professional conversations that keep us energized and learning. We treasure our literate lives and want to pass that along to our students.

9. STAYING IN THE MOMENT

What can separate a teacher's best intentions in delivering the curriculum from the students receiving it is when we think in a future mode. "This will be important for next year," or "You will be expected to know this in fourth grade." Meanwhile the students are tightly sutured to the here and now, finding only the present moment interesting and relevant. The future is later, much, much later. Staying in the moment keeps curriculum more responsive and relevant to students.

Each morning last spring my class raced outside for fifteen minutes of recess. Many students chose to play kickball and took off for the field like they had been handpicked for the Yankees. As I watched them take their turn to kick the ball or catch a pop fly, I marveled at their intensity. Each game held the same significance as the World Series. At first I tried to convince disgruntled and upset young athletes that this was only a game at recess. It wasn't important enough for anger and tears at first base when they were called out. But watching them for a few weeks allowed me to see that each game is "the big game." The only game that counts is the one being played. It doesn't matter if the bleachers are filled with cheering fans or with one lone teacher mesmerized by their fervor. With the purity of childhood, they are in the moment. I stopped trying to persuade kids that their daily game was inconsequential. Instead, I tried to learn what they innately knew and I tended to forget, in my rushed adult way of thinking, that only this moment matters. Make the most of it.

When I wanted students to give their all to a practice test for the state mastery test, I censored myself from the minilecture on the importance of doing well on the test next fall. Instead, we were practicing a test-taking genre. What did they notice about the necessary skills for doing well on each part? Telling them that this experience was something they would need at the beginning of the next year was no more enticing than "when you're older." Instead, I tried to make it interesting and applicable to their lives that day. My long-term view of test-taking would add more anxiety than clarity, so I stuffed it into the closet along with my admonitions to tie their sneakers.

Children naturally think in the present. As adults in a fast-paced world, our thoughts can shoot off like fireworks. *Slowing Down to the Speed of Life* (Carlson and Bailey 1997) substantiates the importance of trying to stay present and in the moment. "When you slow down to the speed of life your perception of the world will change. It will become healthier and easier. You will work more intelligently and wisely than before" (xxii). Although it's another case of easier said than done, it's a worthwhile goal and makes each day feel so much more satisfying.

When children are immersed in good books, they are in the moment, totally engrossed in the now. When they read an assigned story to practice a skill, the shift in emphasis can give the impression that reading this will help them be a better reader in the future. While it is certainly acceptable for children to work toward goals, the possibility of capturing their attention and commitment is greater if the time frame is in the present.

10. APPRECIATING THE COMPLEXITY
OF LEARNING TO READ AND WRITE

As adults take their literacy for granted, it is easy for us to forget the effort and patience it takes to become a reader and a writer. Putting ourselves in the shoes of young learners keeps our teaching responsive and supportive. When we teach from a distance, vital connections between children and their literacy fail to develop.

We need to help kids know that reading and writing are not passive acts, but require full mental participation. Watching a reader in process masks the incredible activity; it is hard to see the intense second-to-second decision making. Readers are aware of the printed text, scanning the words, noticing the punctuation, accessing prior knowledge, hearing the words in their minds, forming interior images, making sense of what the words are saying, predicting the next words or thoughts. This *at-once-ness* is impenetrable to a young nonreader, who sees only pages turning.

Writing looks easy and uncomplicated. Emergent writers see a thoughtful person poised over paper, pencil in hand. What they can't see is how the writer sifts through thoughts, goes backward and forward in his mind, selects the right word, considers the spelling, and writes each letter, while thinking ahead to the next word or the next sentence and maybe jumping back to think about changing what was already written. Inexperienced writers hear a story read aloud and are unaware of the work and revision that went into getting the text just right.

THE NEXT CHAPTER SUGGESTS WAYS I HAVE FOUND TO MODEL the active thinking involved in my own reading and writing. The suggestions demonstrate that my relationship to the reading and writing curriculum is alive and flourishing.

7

Making Our Reading and Writing Visible in the Classroom

olleagues who love to teach reading and writing love books and wondrous words. They read book reviews, make frequent trips to the public library, and enjoy owning their own copy of books they treasure.

"You must read *Frindle* to your class," said Ann Shames, a fifth-grade teacher. "They're going to love it. And you have to read *Ella Enchanted*." If she worked in a bookstore, she couldn't be more of a bookseller. Friends, colleagues, students, and their parents all benefit from Ann's love of a good read.

Enthusiastic readers delight in the well-crafted sentence. They marvel when an author uses ordinary words to express an extraordinary thought. Whether they write for publication or to friends and family on email, their sense of wonder at words gives them an appreciation for those who write well. Along with their bulging canvas school bags, they bring their love of language to school with them each day. And just as their school bags are crammed with school work, their minds are full of books to recommend to their colleagues and students. They promote the skill of book selection and take pride in bringing the right child together with the right book.

Matching the needs of a child to one of the methods in her broad repertoire, the thoughtful and adaptive teacher capitalizes on learning strengths. As they go about the complex task of welcoming children into the literacy club, their range of strategies is fortified by their personal love of reading. This inviolable love permeates the room like the smell of an apple pie in the oven. Their enthusiasm is contagious and they never miss an opportunity to teach children the finer points and pleasures of being a reader and a writer.

Following are a number of practical ways to fold our own love of literacy into the active school day. It's not an exhaustive list but will open the door to ways that show children our commitment to our own literacy growth and theirs. As we work in the teaching and mentoring role with our young apprentices, we all share the rewards of belonging to the literacy club.

READING

My History and Habits as a Reader

The first week of school I tell children my history as a reader. I fell in love with stories when my mother read fairy tales to my sisters and me. I still remember "Little One Eye, Little Two Eye, and Little Three Eye" because it was so frightening. I begged to hear it again and again. Once I could read on my own, I loved the quiet time books gave me away from my nosy and noisy sisters. The summer after fifth grade, the branch library near my house held a reading contest. For each book we read we received a tiny red apple sticker to paste on an eight-inch paper tree. I knew I could be one of the kids with the most apples, and I was. I pedaled my bike fast on the way home from the library. I couldn't wait to start the next Nancy Drew mystery or biography of Abe Lincoln. Each book was a promise of a time ahead when I would lose myself in its pages. My library card was the key to the world outside my neighborhood.

The students in my class know I am still an avid reader. I tell them how I try never to wait in a line, in a car, or at the airport without a book. Sometimes I even brush my teeth or blow my hair dry absorbed in another place and time. Reading weaves in and out of my day, filling the tiny spaces between family and school responsibilities.

Books are the ballast in my busy life. Sometimes I prefer a quick mystery that I can race through, like *"O" Is for Outlaw* by Sue Grafton. Other times I like the kind of book I can savor, like Arthur Golden's *Memoirs of a Geisha*. Then there are times when I read to learn, such as when I read *Brain-Based Learning* by Eric Jensen (1996). I read with highlighter and sticky notes handy, rereading and going back over my highlights. I am also a road reader. I make regular stops at the local library for books on tape. Except when I'm in heavy traffic and need extra concentration, I look forward to having a professional reader entertain me as I drive. I rarely read a book without thinking of a friend or two who must read it next and I am grateful for friends who read with me in mind.

Think Alouds

Students need to see that reading and writing are acts of thinking. Readers and writers may appear still, but their brains are profoundly active. Watching their teacher think aloud while reading or composing short passages or poems helps students see the behind-the-scenes activity implicit in the act of reading and writing. It reminds me of the hilarious play, *Noises Off*. The first act is the dress rehearsal of a mystery as it will be performed on opening night. For the second act, the stage rotates and now the audience sees the frantic activity backstage in order for the actors to give a seamless performance on stage opening night.

So much more is happening during reading and writing than meets the eye. Backstage in the brain, words are decoded or retrieved, images created, questions formulated, prior experiences accessed, ideas connected, and emotions triggered all simultaneously. These acts of literacy, which on the surface appear so uneventful, deserve a standing ovation of respect and appreciation. Watching their teacher think out loud, children learn about the backstage of literacy. It's as eye-opening as a backstage pass.

Modeling what I am thinking as I read shows students what proficient readers do. Using the comprehension strategies described in careful detail in *Mosaic of Thought* (Keene and Zimmermann 1997), I share the thoughts that pass through my head as I am reading. Whether we are focusing on asking questions, or activating schema, or inferring, I know that my modeling makes a difference to the understanding of the students.

As we study different genres during the year, I do repeated demonstrations using that genre. Students watch me think aloud about poetry, non-fiction, biography, and the other genres that we read together. Sometimes I think aloud during a short passage of our chapter read aloud book. I have even done think alouds with student writing. Think alouds help children realize that there is so much more to reading than the words on the page.

Read Aloud

Read aloud is my absolute favorite time of day. It's that welcome deep breath and it is the perfect time to publicly live out my love of reading. I relish reading aloud to a rapt audience who hangs on my every word. It could be I'm just a ham and love the attention, but it's much more than that. I am offering a precious and priceless gift to students. The words of the author combine with my voice and mesmerize them. Time stands still. Pearson's mouth falls open, Jake stares into the distance, Marisa draws tiny rainbows on her paper. Caught up in our imaginations, we have left Room 36 and traveled to another world where all things are possible. And we have gone together—a magical transportation. And every single day students witness my pure pleasure in reading.

Sharing My Reading

I don't want to leave the slightest shadow of a doubt in the minds of the children that I am a truly enthusiastic reader and that I am helping them grow as readers because I believe in the transformational power of books. I have found several easy ways to share what I'm reading with the class and keep them

posted on my personal reading choices. About once a week after a silent reading time (SSR), I invite children to bring their books to the rug and share a
brief thought. I have my book handy and give a few sentences about why I'm
reading it. I want the children to see me as another reader in the group, the
most experienced perhaps, but someone who still faces the same issues all
readers face—particularly, book selection. My resources are the same as the
students: I ask friends for recommendations, I read book reviews, I browse in
libraries and bookstores. When I ask "How do we find books that are right for
us?" I am including myself in the *us*.

When I read *A Life in School* (Tompkins 1996), I took it into class with
me and explained that I was to read it before attending a conference at Bard
College where the author would be the keynote speaker. I showed them how
I had underlined parts I thought I would go back to and the comments I had
written in the margins.

I told the children about the parts of the book I liked and read quickly,
parts where I needed to slow down and reread, and parts where I had questions. As I read the book, I talked to the author and myself. I was eager to keep
reading and discover what Ms. Tompkins knew about teaching from her
unique experience. I didn't feel I had to agree with her, but reading her words
made me think and wonder. That's what I most enjoy from a book and how I
decide if it is worthwhile or not.

As I talked about my reading, my intention was to help these younger
readers know how I interact with the text when I am reading nonfiction. I
bring my own experiences to the book to activate the words on the page.
Without my silent participation, the book is dormant. Just as musical notes
on a page are silent until they are played or sung, words on a page are silent
until joined to our thoughts.

After the two-day conference at Bard College with Jane Tompkins,
I showed the class the twenty-eight pages of notes and writing I had done.
I explained how I had gone back through my notes and highlighted parts I
wanted to remember. I used sticky notes to mark passages I wanted to talk
about with colleagues.

If I am reading a book that might interest the class, I read a short passage
to them. *Endurance* (Lansing 1999), the story of Shakleton's attempt to cross
Antarctica by land, was one such book and I choose a particularly gripping
part to share. I clip articles from the newspaper or magazines to read aloud or
summarize. They see me tape short articles into my journal, exchange books
with other teachers, or swap quick book recommendations. They know I belong to a book club that meets once a month, what book we are reading, and
how well I enjoy it. In other words, my reading habits are visible. I read three
hundred and sixty-five days a year. I don't have a "vacation literacy" where I

only find time to read when school's not in session. Reading sustains me, brings me pleasure, keeps me informed. If someone asked the students in my class to name three people who love to read, I am confident that my name would be on the top of that list.

WRITING

At first it can seem a little trickier to share writing with the class, especially if we don't think of ourselves as writers. Nevertheless, if I want to sell the importance and pleasure of writing to the students, I must own it myself and show them that I do. As Don Graves writes in *A Fresh Look at Writing*,

> You, the teacher, are the most important factor in creating a learning environment in the classroom. Your students will observe how you treat writing in your own life, how you learn, and what is important to you through the questions you ask of the world around you. How you demonstrate values, how you knowledgeably show the meaning of writing as a craft, will have a profound effect on their learning. (109)

Sharing My Writing

I happen to be someone who enjoys writing articles for teachers and stories and poems for children. That makes it easy for me to demonstrate that I write. Every few weeks I'll take a turn during group share to ask for help with one of my stories or poems. When I read my story and ask for ideas, I am sincerely inviting their suggestions. Later I'll share my revisions with them and show how I have incorporated their comments and questions. The strategies that I use for revision they can try in their own writing.

Note-Taking

For teachers who do not have the time or inclination to write, there are still ways to show children how and why we write. Note-taking is one such way. I take notes because it helps me remember information better and I like to go back to what I've written to refresh my memory. Note-taking is a habit for me and one worth demonstrating to children. When the children share observations and ideas during class discussions, I make notes so I can remember their words. I have a record of their thoughts and they realize what they say is important enough for me to write it in my journal. When the class attends an assembly, I tuck my journal under my arm so I can jot down information I don't want to forget. Later, when we talk about the assembly, I use my notes as a reminder. Students see me refer to my notes and use that information. When the school nurse does her energetic presentation on germs or Officer Friendly talks about the local police, I sit at my desk and take a few notes rather than correcting math papers. This makes it easier to refer back to the information later and demonstrates to students a way to extend learning through note-taking. Sometimes I take notes on an overhead transparency so I can show the class what I noticed and how I organized the information. Note-taking is a skill some students embrace more readily than others, just as adults vary in their need to jot notes. Observing their teacher take and refer to notes sets the stage for later school life when learning and note-taking go hand in hand.

Jotting Ideas

How do we get everyone to participate when we brainstorm ideas and create a reference chart? How do we get everyone thinking before the discussion? We ask them to write *and* the teacher jots her ideas, too. I used to start a reference chart by calling everyone to the circle. Then the extroverts took over and the rest of the class could coast while the children who loved to share dominated the discussion. Asking children to jot down a few ideas before we begin sharing ideas pushes all children to begin thinking about the topic. The discussion acquires added value when the teacher is one of the participating members of the group who shares what she wrote.

Journal Entries

Journals have become a given in the school setting. Asking children to think on paper is now the norm. It supports children in their journal efforts if their teacher keeps a journal as well. Sometimes I make a journal entry in my journal and at other times I'll write an entry on the white board or chart paper so the students can see me composing. They seem to take the assignment more seriously when I am writing with them. It is also important for them to see how I think as I write and work to match my intentions to what I write.

Sometimes when I write my journal entry for them to see, we take time to talk about what they notice in my entry. What makes it a good entry? What would make it better? My journal write is an authentic attempt to express my opinion and this captures their interest more than a staged exercise. Repeated discussions throughout the year continually raise the bar on journal expectations. One discussion doesn't do it. I spiral back to it and keep my expectations explicit and gently growing.

Weekend News

Weekend news is another opportunity to demonstrate writing skills and strategies. It also changes the energy in the room when I write alongside my students. The quiet music starts and I pick up my journal and settle into a seat—maybe near Sean, who needs my supportive presence after a demanding weekend, or next to Jordan, who finds writing arduous and prefers the company of someone who believes in him.

Sometimes I'll write my weekend news on an overhead transparency so children can critique it with me. What would they like to know more about? What details seem to be missing? Which part grabs their attention? They enjoy learning more about my time away from the classroom and helping me with revisions.

Students understand that adults need uninterrupted time to write, too. When they observe me faithfully writing and sketching in my journal, they see it as an authentic way in which I keep track of my life. My journal is concrete evidence that writing enriches my life.

Writing to a Prompt

Writing to a prompt is part of our fourth-, sixth-, and eighth-grade state mastery test and something children practice several times a year. Like our former story-starter writing program of the early 1980s, children write for forty-five minutes about an assigned topic. It is easy to underestimate what a challenging task that is. Writing to the prompt along with the students gives me a true appreciation for the complexities of writing an organized story with a beginning, middle, and end at one sitting. Whoa! It's not easy to do well. The conversation around our written responses is richer when I am struggling, too.

Finding strategies for writing a better story in a test setting is a task we problem solve together. I *do* tell them strategies for writing to a prompt, but incorporating those strategies into a forty-five minute exercise is a horse of a different color. It's like the discrepancy between telling someone how to dive and actually going off the board and getting wet. My stance toward the task would be more officious if I hadn't tried writing to the prompt myself. I would be giving advice in a vacuum. Students realize that the act of writing a finished piece in one sitting is challenging even for an experienced writer and their attitude during the discussion takes on an added seriousness and purpose. We are figuring this out together. My legitimate not-knowing allows students to assume more of the adult role.

Thank-You Notes

There are so many occasions and reasons to thank people in our school and community. When Mr. Caruso, our custodian, replaces the closet handle, we compose a quick note of thanks together on chart paper. When the firemen come to talk to the class about fire safety, their time and expertise also deserves a written thank-you. These notes don't require fancy prose, but are another chance for children to see how the written word plays a purposeful role in our daily lives. Composing them together is another opportunity for modeling writing strategies and skills.

Composing Together

I look for other opportunities for the class to compose together. As we write our class views about the new playground rules to the student council, for example, they see how an adult writer takes the ideas and works them into clear, understandable sentences. As I offer different ways to express the same idea, students watch an experienced writer manipulating language. They offer their opinions about wording and sentence order. What makes the most sense? Is there a better way to say this? Composing together demonstrates strategies students can use in their own writing, such as sentence combining, using transitional words, and adding interesting details.

After we compose a letter together, I type it up on the computer or ask for a student volunteer who's in the mood to type. Students can relax as we compose together knowing they won't have to copy all those words on their own later. This group writing goes up on the wall for future shared readings, as a spelling reference, and a writing model. Composing together is a time when we share ideas and experiment with expressing ourselves well.

Class Newsletter

Over the years I have had a number of different kinds of newsletters that go home to parents on a regular basis. One year the class brainstormed events from the week on Friday morning while I typed them up. Two children were assigned to be the editors of the draft. While the class had art I made revisions and ran off copies to go home.

A first-grade teacher, Jacque O'Brien, meets each day with her class at the chart stand before dismissal. They suggest three or four sentences about the day's activities. She copies down their words on the chart and then types up their sentences from Monday through Thursday. On Friday, the children glue the sheet from Monday through Thursday onto the left-hand side of their letter journal and add their own sentences about Friday on the right-hand side.

The journal then goes home over the weekend for parents to write back. Composing together at the end of each day, while the teacher writes their words, provides a comfortable routine and gives young students daily practice in thinking on paper together.

Classroom Memories

Writing memories about the year is another time when I model how I choose my memory and compose it. Students are just as curious about what stands out in my memory as I am about what they choose. Jennifer Barnard, a second-grade teacher, found a way for children to reflect at the end of each month. Folding five legal-size pieces of paper one over the other, she creates one long book with ten extending tabs. At the end of each month, the children write the name of the month on the tab or divider and then draw and write about their memories from the month. She also uses what they write as a time for them to assess their own progress. The important extension is that Jen also writes her memories and highlights her process with the class. Watching a skilled adult think out loud about how to translate ideas into words on the page proves more profitable than ten worksheets on "How to Organize Your Writing."

Poetry

I love writing poems for my class because they are such a good audience. They can discriminate OK from terrible, but seem to enjoy whatever I write, especially if it rhymes. If I want children to like poetry, reading lots and lots of poems with them is one way. The added hook is when I write poems as well.

Two years ago we had an amazingly mild winter. I loved not worrying about icy roads driving to school, but I had to admit by March, a snow day would have been a delicious treat. Low and behold! April first I woke up to six inches of fluffy, white snow covering my backyard. I stood at the kitchen counter and wrote:

APRIL FIRST

I can finally build a snowman!
The snow's so deep and thick.
I pack it with my mittens.
I can tell that it will stick.

I gently shape a little ball
Then roll it on the ground.
Kneeling down I pack more snow.
The ball grows fat and round.

My older sister helps me
Lift each cold and lumpy ball.
We pat more snow around the neck
So the wobbly head won't fall.

He's ready for his carrot nose
And wood chips for his eyes.
My *first* snowman this winter
What an April Fool's surprise!

I enjoyed the rest of my unexpected snow day. The next day I told the class how I had stood at the kitchen counter to write down the poem that popped into my head. One thing I know for sure about poems—like shiny soap bubbles, if I don't write them down immediately, they quickly disappear.

I showed the class my three pages of rough draft and read them my poem. It still didn't satisfy me. I needed their help and suggestions. In the version I read to them, the fourth verse said:

He's ready for his carrot nose
And a bubble pipe to smoke
My *first* snowman this winter
What an April Fool's Day joke!

I was uncomfortable with my snowman smoking. What else could I describe on the snowman that would allow me to rhyme the last sentence in a way that made sense? Iliana figured out that "surprise" could be the last word, because it was a big surprise to have our first snowfall in April. That would rhyme with eyes. What would I use for eyes on a snowman? Stones? Charcoal? David waved his hand in the air. "We used wood chips yesterday," he said. "Wood chips it is!" I replied.

The children were a delightful and delighted sounding board as I moved words around, crossed some out, changed the number of syllables. The poem's still not ready for an anthology, but asking the class for help inspired several students to try their hand at writing poetry. When the teacher writes a less than perfect poem, it somehow grants children permission to give it a go. That's the way they find out they have poems inside, too.

Art and Writing

My school district is so fortunate to have Dr. Karen Ernst daSilva on our staff. Karen has helped us learn about the power of art in writing. When she first worked with teachers at Kings Highway School as the art teacher (she had previously taught eighth-grade English), she invited them to join their classes in the art room and participate with the children. Teachers began carrying sketch journals and using them in the classroom. Then they passed their excitement on to the students who began to observe closely, sketch patiently, and write about their drawings. Amazing things happened because Karen had the courage to break the mold and to invite teachers to reinvent themselves as artists and writers.

In my first after-school Artists-Writers Workshop with twenty-five other teachers, Karen gave us an hour and a half to work on something we would really like to try. We were to write about our process and discoveries before we met to share. An hour and a half to do a project in the art room? What could I do for that long? My initial sense of inadequacy mushroomed as classmates started milling around. The momentum of everyone else getting busy forced me to make a decision. Here is the reflection I wrote at the end of the work time:

> I chose this art card (van Gogh's *Irises*) because I like to draw flowers and thought I'd have at least a small shot at imitating it. Yikes! No sooner had I started than I realized my paper was too large. I couldn't handle drawing and changing proportions to a larger size.
>
> But I need to back up. I chose to sit off alone because I knew I needed more quiet and I was also intimidated by the course veterans. I didn't want to be distracted by worry and comparison. In other words, I was seven years old again.
>
> Another way I knew I was seven was that I knew when I finished I wanted someone to tell me how much they liked my picture. Even as I struggled with the initial pencil marks, I sensed my inner child hoping for praise. Was I just feeling vulnerable?
>
> First I sketched the pitcher and leaves. As I tried to tackle the iris flowers, I lost patience and confidence. I decided I didn't have to be faithful to van Gogh's purple flowers and settled for a shortcut.
>
> Once I had sketched the art card in pencil, I went over the lines with pen. Then realizing my original idea of watercolor just went out the window because I had used a pen (the ink would run) instead of permanent marker, I decided to use crayons. I think that worked better anyway.

We sat on the floor in a circle, showed our artwork, and talked or read about our process. Several kind colleagues made positive comments about my artistic attempt. Actually, it did look rather lovely. The best part, however, was what we learned from each other. I wasn't the only one who returned to childhood and that sense of fear and adventure. I understood so clearly why creating art and writing alongside students is magical and transforming.

Walking in the shoes of our students keeps us fresh and alive. Learning sharpens our teaching. A large painted sign in the art room says ". . . imagine what you most would like to do to help keep the world magical." Drawing, writing, and taking risks along with students is one way.

JOINING OUR STUDENTS IN THEIR LEARNING AND LITERACY processes heightens their awareness and ours. Constructing knowledge together takes the artificial lid off the learning kettle. The sky's the limit. Teacher participation as a mentor and fellow learner encourages a stronger, more resilient sense of community. When the teacher wants all students to know the magic of reading and writing as she does, her relationship to the curriculum is one of authentic example.

8

The Relationship Between Students and Curriculum

*S*chool started last week. Rained poured from the sky as students poured off the buses and into the building. Their tentative faces spoke volumes about this place called elementary school. Some children grasped the hand of a sibling or friend and reminded me of Hansel and Gretel venturing into the deep, dark woods. Some children looked like Cinderella at the ball, radiant and expectant. A new year of learning, listening, following directions, and behaving loomed or glistened ahead.

Questions drifted in the air as the children shuffled by. Will I like my teacher? Will my teacher like me? Will I like the kids in my class? Will they like me? Will I be able to learn what I'm supposed to?

What a variety of children flowed past: different sizes, shapes, colors, attitudes, clothing choices, even gait. How do we successfully help all these young learners, I wondered. Thirty years ago I would have answered my own question with a simple reply: by teaching-telling them what we want them to know. During my maiden voyage as a teacher, I tended to equate teaching with learning. If I did my part, teach-tell, and they did their part, learn-listen, we could cover the curriculum and live happily ever after.

Such magical thinking is possible in any fairy tale. But in real life there is no simple equation between teaching and learning. Our brains are as unique as our smiles. With the information we now have available to us about brain-based learning, multiple intelligences, personality types, and learning styles, we have the potential to create even better bonds between students and the curriculum. As we uncover the learning profile of each child, we increase the likelihood that all children will make that lifelong connection to reading and writing.

In *The Courage to Teach,* Parker J. Palmer describes this as one of the most difficult truths about teaching. "What we teach will never 'take' unless it connects with the inward core of our students' lives" (1998, 31).

The curriculum diet we offer children invites them to share in a rich banquet or a handful of stale crackers and hardened cheese. Through planning and organization, teachers create opportunities for students to find numerous points of entry into the literate life. A classroom context alive with pursuits that appeal to kids and promote their development as readers and writers sparks their inner fire. This internal shift transforms them. Reading and writing are no longer school activities, but deep in their bones.

Most children place great faith in their teachers. They will try their best to do whatever is asked of them:

Read a story and then answer the questions?
OK.
Do this silently and alone?
OK.
Sit in a small group and talk about a story that I don't really like?
OK.
Do this again tomorrow?
Well, OK, I guess so.
Do this over and over again for months?
Well, OK, if I have to.
Do this again next year with a different teacher and kids?
I hope not.
Read when it's not assigned?
No thanks.

How we groom students to become enthusiastic readers and writers depends on the relationships we invite and allow between each child and the curriculum. Just as teachers must own the curriculum before it hums a happy tune, students must see, feel, understand, and connect to it as well. The workshop format allows diverse learners to discover their own way of connecting to reading and writing. The structure of the workshop invites children to participate in ways that meet their needs. Thoughtfully adaptive teachers present short and targeted lessons; then, while kids are engaged in reading and writing that is important to them, the teacher is able to confer with individuals and in small groups. Meeting together at the end of the workshop offers another opportunity for children to learn, from both teacher and student input. This daily closure is a time of assessment and celebration for hard work accomplished.

Workshops provide bounded flexibility so qualities necessary to literacy connections can be encouraged. What characteristics of the classroom serve children best in their growth as joyfully literate human beings? What conditions give them a sense that they are of consequence in the classroom and that their contribution and participation with the curriculum make a difference to them and the class? How do we create resilient relationships for all students with the reading and writing curriculum? Below is my list of conditions for students to thrive as readers and writers. These overarching conditions are the basics in an effective and engaging reading and writing classroom.

CONDITIONS THAT BUILD LASTING RELATIONSHIPS BETWEEN STUDENTS AND CURRICULUM

Experiential Knowledge

Words are limited in what they can teach. Our most lasting learning comes from our own experiences. Explaining to a six-month-old how to walk sounds silly. And yet we expect children to learn important lessons from our verbal instructions about life. The lessons that stay with us are the ones that seep into our bodies and our understanding from our own experimentation and actions. Learning comes from experiences and discovering their meanings and lessons in our own lives.

As Eric Jensen writes in *Brain-Based Learning* (1996), "While it's true that much learning can occur without ever leaving a seat, it's true that most of what you think is important in your life, what you 'really know,' you have learned through experience, not from a chalkboard or textbook" (100).

What does this mean as students learn each day? Young learners need to experience what it means to be a reader and writer in a real world way, not just in a school way. They need time to read and time to write, time to talk about reading and talk about writing. They work to improve as readers and writers but much of their class time is spent reading, not practicing skills in isolation. Through shared and guided reading with the teacher and with reading buddies, students grow as readers in the process of reading. They grow as writers in the process of writing. Direct instruction connects to the act of reading or writing and the skills and strategies are relevant and appropriate at that point in time.

In *Human Brain and Human Learning*, Leslie Hart emphasizes the importance of learning by doing. "When we define learning as the acquisition of useful programs, we illuminate to the fullest the hopelessness of lecturing. No programs can be built by listening, but only by acting in some fashion"

(1983, 134). Daily experiences of being readers and writers lead to the formation of habits of the mind necessary to lifelong literacy.

When my daughter, Sara, was in third grade back in the early eighties, she thought reading in school meant the reading period scheduled each morning. It was the ninety minutes when she read a story in a basal reader and filled in pages in a workbook. She sat at a table with four or five other children and answered the teacher's questions and corrected the workbook pages. Reading wasn't a time to learn how to make book choices or to read beyond the assigned story. It was a school subject that happened each day at the same time in the same way. It wasn't a real-world pursuit with promises of lifelong learning and pleasure. It was an hour and a half to be endured.

Many young students today experience reading in school as the act of reading real books. They talk about what they read and practice the habits of proficient readers. Their daily experiences as readers and writers reinforce these habits. When the books they read are at that "just-right" reading level for them, their confidence, interest, and pleasure take root. Being an accomplished reader and writer is an aspiration. As a child curls up with a savory story, he anticipates many such opportunities ahead. The experience of reading feels right and worthwhile.

"Learning and meaning is driven by feelings: The brain is virtually a 'box of emotions,'" writes Eric Jensen. "While we can be presented with evidence that something is true, it is not verified in our own world until we *feel* that it is true" (1996, 29). No matter how many times we tell children that reading and writing are valuable and pleasurable enterprises, until they experience that for themselves our words ring hollow. Their daily reading and writing habits give them the experiences to know it is true for them.

"I love this book!" Elana exclaimed after SSR. "Do we have any other books by Jennifer Armstrong?"

"I'm almost to the end of the chapter. Can I finish it before I come to the circle?" Katrina pleads. "I have to find out what's going to happen!"

"I was right there with Buddy in the hold of the ship," Jason reported. "I forgot I was in school." We chuckled.

"Reading's great, isn't it?" I said.

When children experience the power of reading and writing firsthand, their relationship to literacy blossoms and that connection gently grows more substantial with each text read or written.

Choice

Choice enlivens our existence and grants us the chance to make decisions and try new things. Choice with responsibility is the backbone of our democracy. It must have its tender roots in the classrooms of young learners. Children need opportunities to know the pleasure of making wise choices and the disappointment of the wrong ones. Through the decision making and responsibility that choices allow, children develop the confidence to discover who they are.

Choices in the reading/writing classroom keep children participating and engaged. Burnout can happen at any age, even to children. Motivation and energy hinge on choices. Seemingly small choices add a spark to an assignment. When choices allow students to make assignments compatible with their own goals in learning, they work with the flow of their energy. Julia asks to modify the reading response assignment and I respond with an enthusiastic "Yes!" I watch her demeanor brighten and her posture straighten. Pursuing her very own idea feels so much freer and empowering than connecting the teacher's dots. A few children prefer the security of lock-step directions, but with support they too can begin to make independent decisions.

During reading workshop, children can learn to make wise choices about

- which book to read for independent reading
- which child to work with for partner reading
- which books to read by the author being studied
- what subject to research during a nonfiction study
- which kind of response to write about (e.g., character, setting, connections to text, problem/solution, etc.)
- where to sit during independent reading
- where to sit during chapter book read aloud
- what materials to use for drawing a reading response
- whether to continue or abandon a book selected for independent reading
- what their goals and intentions are as they read

During writing workshop, children learn to make deliberate choices about:

- what kind of materials to use for writing
- whether to draw a picture
- the topic for their writing
- how long their story will be

- if they want to read their writing for group share
- which pieces to revise and publish

This list just scratches the surface. Children often ask questions that lead to other legitimate choices. A choice is a vote of confidence by the teacher. It encodes the message that you have a valuable and thoughtful opinion and are a responsible decision maker. A choice says, "I trust and respect you" and shows appreciation for individual preferences.

Leslie Hart, in *Human Brain and Human Learning*, writes: "When students are always told what to do, the tendency is strong for those who give the orders to set objectives too low for many students. But in settings where students have more room to choose their own, they can often be startling in their originality and level" (1983, 134). Choices elevate classroom activities, motivate learners, and allow students to surprise us with their thinking. Choices invite children to have their own wonderful ideas, a definite way to build their link to literacy.

When children choose between lined and unlined paper for their writing, the unlined paper they select seems to offer more possibilities. It is human nature to feel more connected to things we choose. Choosing forces a decision and an action. It makes us more aware, more alive. Prescribed programs with each step predetermined are restrictive. It's like wearing a shirt two sizes too small. There is no room to wiggle and stretch.

Choices are an integral aspect of reading and writing. Which book do I read? Which story do I tell? When children are taught to read and write without practice in making responsible choices, their relationship to literacy is jeopardized. For students to make a lifelong connection to books, choice must be an inherent component of their reading habits. Children who do not have a choice about what to read or write are less likely to do either on their own. Their relationship to reading and writing will be strictly on a need-to-do basis.

Time

Time is one of our most valuable resources in school. There never seems to be enough of it, except maybe the week before spring vacation. How do teachers fit all they are supposed to teach into the tight timetable? It's so easy to get caught up in the frenzy and fast pace of our society. Everything is on fast forward. Yet we know that learning has its own pace, just as children have their own developmental rhythms and patterns.

I absolutely do *not* want to rush children in the classroom and I probably do it more than I realize. Slowing down, giving children a chance to think, a chance to do their best—this is a goal I try to keep in the foreground. As a teacher talks with students during the day in a variety of interactions, her focus creates the illusion of infinite time. Her patient presence and listening speaks volumes about the pace. The message is clear: "We have time for you to do your best thinking and work." The hurries and worries of the rest of the world do not creep under the classroom door.

The allocation of time during the school day has an impact on the relationships students forge with the curriculum. Here are my priorities for what children deserve each day:

- Time to talk and be listened to—with adults, with their peers, individually and in groups, formally and informally, in focused and brainstorming conversations. Talking helps learning become long-term.
- Time to read—time with book in hand to read for a purpose or pleasure, but uninterrupted time to live the reader's life.
- Time to write—time to think on paper about learning or time to try out ideas from their imagination.
- Time to reflect—time to look back at work from the period, day, week, and/or month to celebrate growth and set goals.
- Time to become immersed in a project—time to plan and execute a more involved project that allows for exploration of possibilities, solves problems, and brings efforts to fruition.
- Time to listen to fine literature (of all genres)—time to be surrounded with stimulating language as the teacher reads aloud from carefully chosen texts.
- Time to think, wonder, and challenge themselves—time to use imagination and set high goals.

It is easy to let the pace of the classroom feel like the hall at dismissal. In our hurry to cover the curriculum, activities become the daily diet and teaching for understanding gets lost in the paper shuffle. Reexamining how we allocate time each day and eliminating busywork activities that don't contribute to literacy connections frees up time for what matters. Integrating subjects is another way astute teachers have found to give the day more breathing room.

Time spent doing what's essential for literacy allows students to relate to the curriculum in a meaningful way. Without time to experience what it feels like to be a reader and a writer, a strong connection between students and literacy just won't happen. We demonstrate what we value in our classrooms by giving it attention and time. A child's relationship to literacy deserves both.

Enriching Environments

Enriched environments not only look more interesting and inviting, they make a difference in how well children learn. Brain research with rats indicates that an enriched environment helps them grow thicker and more numerous dentrites. Studies with humans have verified the effect of an environment filled with colorful posters, affirmations, and opportunities for social interactions—it boosts learning (Jensen 1996, 55).

Some teachers are so creative with space and supplies. Through long hours before school starts, they transform a lifeless institutional room into a welcoming, comfortable setting for maximum learning. Bookshelves with books sorted and coded, materials available for artwork and exploration, these and other thoughtful displays set the stage for intimacy, inquiry, and rigor. Small spaces invite children to curl up and focus in a special niche. A rug signals a place to come together to share and learn. Word walls and bulletin boards with reference charts and shared writing are added during the year and provide resources for spelling and models of writing.

But just as a house is not a home, a beautifully decorated classroom is not necessarily an enriching environment. It must also be a place where there is more than one right answer, where there is more than one solution and multiple ways to think about books and issues. An enriched environment has spaces for playfulness, for laughter, for compassion, for honest emotions. It is a place that honors the uniqueness of everyone who enters and encourages collaboration and growth. Social interaction and a strong sense of community support the learning process. Trust, commitment, and pride are the special curtains that drape the room. Respect and caring are the lights that shine from all eyes.

An enriched environment allows time for Ethan to pursue his love of writing, for Jessica to read all the books by Bill Britain, and for Marc and Seth to partner read their way through the books of John Bellairs. Explicit learning outcomes guide the way, but understanding of learning styles and multiple intelligences provide choices for success. The teacher models her learning and thinking, but recognizes the individual preferences and needs of her students. In these classrooms, it's not "My way or the highway." There are multiple ways to achieve the learning outcomes.

In *Human Brain and Human Learning,* Leslie Hart writes:

> Suppose we give 25 jigsaw puzzles, all the same, to 25 students, whether children or adults. Each will put the pieces together in a different sequence and at varying speeds; but given time, all will likely complete it. . . . Once we grasp the individual way that human brains extract patterns, we can begin to see the futility of offering a standardized, limited input. (78)

A classroom environment that honors these differences offers an invitation to all children to forge a solid connection to the reading and writing curriculum.

A recent experience in an after school Artists-Writers Workshop surprised me and taught me firsthand about the fascinating way our brains tune in to things in the environment. I sat a stool away from Jen Barnard, a second-grade teacher, as we worked on our artwork. I was trying to paint a large turtle from an illustration in a picture book. On my left, Jen was painting a winter landscape. I wasn't paying much attention to her. In order to draw I had to focus on details in the picture and concentrate on each one. I wasn't even aware of the medium Jen was using.

A few days later I came across a poem about winter that I had written several years ago—my simple "Ode to Winter":

> It's dark outside at five o'clock.
> My fingers sting inside my gloves.
> My breath comes out in tiny clouds.
> That's winter for you.
>
> The days are short and end too soon.
> Darkness crowds the daylight hours.
> I only want to stay indoors.
> That's winter for you.
>
> Yes, that's winter for you.
> It's not for me.

I decided to add my poem to my poetry journal and mount it on a winter background. When my class went to art, I sat at a table with students and thought about how to make a winter night sky. I decided to draw white crayon dots on the paper and then to watercolor over them in blue and purple. The crayon relief gave just the right look. Once the paint dried, I glued the painting into my journal and added the poem that I had typed in a dark blue font. The poem stood out against the dark winter sky with falling snow. I felt quite accomplished.

The following Wednesday at the next teacher class, we met in a circle on the rug to share out artwork from the previous week. When Jen held up her winter picture my mouth fell open. There was exactly the winter sky that I had made. When the sharing ended I walked over to Jen.

"I want to show you something," I said. "Open your journal to your picture again, please."

She did and I held up the winter page I had done a few days earlier. The snowy skies in our pictures were identical. "How did you do yours?" I asked Jen.

"I used white crayon and water color," she said. "Why?"

"I had no idea that I was copying what you had done last week, until I saw it today!" I explained. "When I decided to do this winter sky, I thought the idea just came out of the blue. I must have noticed you in my peripheral vision without even realizing it. There is too big a similarity to be a coincidence."

Jen smiled. "Wow!"

"I know. Brain research says we learn from things around us, the peripherals on the wall, and so on. I never really thought about how we learn *unknowingly* from the people around us."

"That means kids learn from the others in the class without even being aware of it. Spooky." Jen added with a laugh.

Jen and I got to work on our next project. What I had done trailed through my thoughts. It wasn't just an accident that I had copied Jen. On some deeper level I had learned from her about how to paint an evening winter sky.

I tell this story because it speaks to how we learn. What we learn is not just what we are told or what we read or what we consciously experience. There are hidden levels to our learning, things we surreptitiously tuck away in our brains. When I think about all that humans learn, this makes sense. There is no possible way we could know all we do if we weren't picking up information from our total environment all the time.

While trying to clear some of the papers and clutter in my office, I uncovered notes from Caine and Caine's *Making Connections: Teaching and the Human Brain* that I had written while reading the book in the summer of 1994. Note number seven says: "Learning involves both focused attention and peripheral perception." Note number eight reads: "Learning always involves conscious and unconscious processes." I had never doubted these statements to be true, but I had to experience them in such an obvious way to truly comprehend them.

Right away I think about what this means in the classroom. Children learn not only what we are trying to teach and what they are trying to learn, but also from what other students are doing, what hangs on the walls, what sits on the shelves. In a rich environment, they learn far more than they are taught. When students live in an enriching literate environment surrounded by young readers and writers reading real books and engaged in full-fledged authoring, they are marinating in the sauce of lifelong literacy. The positive energy that flows from reader to reader helps to ignite the reading spark in all children. The curriculum we offer to students must be more like lace than polyester, with spaces for their own light to shine through. Then their relationship to literacy can have its own intricate pattern and design. Because it begins inside the child it will be an organic and vigorous relationship, not just a tenuous connection based on assignments and external requirements.

Opportunities for Long Thinking

Last February I asked students to bring in ten photos from their life that represented their personal history. They would arrange their photos on large poster board, write a draft of captions, and then type up their final copy on the computer in their favorite font.

The next morning as the first bell rang, I wished for five more minutes of quiet time. Then Paige soared through the door eager to share pictures of when she was a baby, a toddler, hugging her dog, laughing with her brother. Seeing Paige as a young child made me fall in love with her all over again. What a little cutie she had been! What an energy boost her photographs brought to her classmates and me.

"Oh, Paige! You were so adorable!" Carrie cooed, pointing at Paige next to a pumpkin.

"I had that same stuffed puppy," Jason said, looking over her shoulder.

As they arrived each day, the children happily perused each others' photos. Later in the day they spread out around the room to plan their posters. They asked each other questions and told stories about their snapshots. A natural rapport permeated the room as the children relaxed and worked on this project. It didn't have to be done today. It could take as long as needed to make it their best. Some children finished in three or four work periods. Others needed almost twice that much time.

Working on a project for several days or several weeks or even months shifts the energy and pace in the room. Students work independently and follow their own intuitive sense as they plan and execute their project. Some children find this style of work perfect for their personality and learning style. Others need more support along the way. But all children benefit from the chance to take an idea, come at it from different angles, and bring their plan to fruition.

Whenever the children in my class have engaged in long-term projects, their excitement and commitment are palpable. Whether researching information about the Northeast states, bats, or biographies, students welcome the chance to spread their wings and tackle a long-range project in class. Projects completed at home are not the same. I like to be able to make the steps of the learning adventure explicit and, like a Border Collie, keep some sheep from wandering off or straggling behind. Recently I've learned reasons that make these projects more than fun activities that kids enjoy. I always sensed they were good for children. Now I know why.

"Activate the brain through presentations, skits, mock debates, *Jeopardy* shows, and humorous treatments of commercials. Include creative and/or entertaining activities as a regular part of the learning process" (153), recommends Eric Jensen in *Brain-Based Learning*. Research supports the effectiveness of creative presentations where students have the opportunity to reach multiple goals: social, artistic, emotional, and academic (153).

In *Methods That Matter*, Harvey Daniels and Marilyn Bizar explain that "Representing to Learn" is one of six key methods that matter. "All contemporary learning theories share one precept: in order for students to remember information, they must act on it" (1998, 96). Representing what they have learned through writing or art is a way learning becomes permanent.

There are six ways for students to represent their learning, but those branch out into an infinite number of possibilities. Teachers have been utilizing these ideas for years to culminate a learning unit, as a means of assessment and/or celebration. Students can represent their learning by:

- writing—stories, letters, journal entries, poems
- drawing—pictures, book illustrations, graphic designs, masks, maps
- oral presentations—drama, recitation, puppet shows
- other visual methods—diagrams, models, posters, mobiles
- other artistic methods—compose a song, paint a picture, sculpt a clay representation
- kinesthetically—choreograph a dance, create movements to accompany a story or poem

Given a choice of ways to make their learning permanent, students are able to follow their own interests, talents, and passions. The result over time, with monitoring and support, is an incredible sense of pride and accomplishment.

Long-term projects give children an opportunity to learn the important ability to make a plan and follow through on it. It also lets students delve deeply into a topic that they care about, where their curiosity pulls them to more and better questions, where the energy for the project is generated intrinsically by the student, not the assignment.

The school day is filled with many quick journeys that are like a trip to the grocery store for milk. Longer journeys invite children to be explorers— to make wrong turns, retrace their tracks, and make a commitment to something that is not attainable in one sitting. These longer journeys allow students to develop the lifelong skills of thinking ahead, thinking deeply, and getting lost in the pleasure of learning. They also give kids a chance to create their own special relationship to literacy. The chance to think long and deeply about a facet of reading or writing invites children to savor the benefits of the literacy club. Without frequent opportunities to veer from the path and blaze their own trail, personal connections to literacy remain fragile at best. The passion, playfulness, and pleasure children bring to a project helps them to form a lasting literacy bond as they work hard on something they truly care about.

Reflection and Metacognition

It's taken me years to see my own patterns as a learner. How do I learn new information? What tweaks my curiosity? Which learning situations overwhelm me? Young readers and writers benefit from paying attention to their strengths and weaknesses as they forge a solid relationship with reading and writing. Reflecting on their habits as a reader and writer, pausing to consider growth over time, and noticing not only what they are learning but their thinking about it is a keystone of their learning foundation and their connection to long-term literacy.

Four second graders and I met to talk about their preferences as readers. Able to read books at a higher level than many of their classmates, their fondest desire was to be left alone to read. They were unanimous that talking and writing about books just took precious time away from reading.

"Do you know why readers talk about books?" I asked, studying their earnest faces.

"To know if we read it right," Lauren said.

I had predicted that answer. Talking about books is to prove to the teacher that students understand what they read. Their reading experience so far had not included conversations that added to their understanding of a book or of differing opinions. Certainly, their desire to read will serve them well and already provides them with hours of pleasure—but what I would wish for them and all young readers is to realize the many facets of reading that stretch and enliven its appeal.

As students' skills and strategies develop, so should their understanding of themselves as readers. This elevates them to the next level, that of the aware reader. Aware readers choose to read and can handle a variety of genres with good comprehension and memory. Another level of awareness also sets them apart—their metacognition. They think about their reading. Aware readers are:

- aware of what it means to be a reader and of reading's power and potential in their lives
- aware that they are meaning makers

- aware that they have a repertoire of strategies for understanding and remembering text
- aware that readers see, feel, understand, and connect to the text
- aware that other readers may interpret the text differently
- aware of using their imaginations as they read
- aware that talking, drawing, and/or writing about a text deepens understanding and remembering
- aware that reading improves through reading

When I was a reading teacher in a closet back in the 1970s, the goal my principal set for me each year was that my students read on grade level by June. That, of course, meant that students needed to achieve a grade-level score on the end-of-the-year standardized test. What an incredibly low standard we set then. Passing a test doesn't tell us whether a child chooses to read, has the ability to select appropriate books, or has an awareness of the metacognitive aspects of being a reader. Today's young readers deserve a bigger bag of intellectual tools. Taking a step back and looking at themselves as readers invites kids to appraise their progress and set goals for themselves. It sends the message that the decisions they make as a reader are of significance. This empowering stance supports their growing tie to the literate world.

Writing is a way for students to discover deeper levels of their thinking. When the words flow onto the page, writers get to thoughts buried beneath the surface of their lives. I learned this again when I joined a high school English class as an observer and participant. The class started with journal writing. The topic: What is your favorite day of the week? I opened by journal and got right to work. Of course, I knew my favorite day of the week. It was Friday. As I wrote during the next ten minutes, I made an amazing discovery: Thursday was really my favorite. As the prelude to Friday, it was filled with hopeful anticipation. I sat and considered what I had written. Yes, I had to agree with myself. I *did* find Thursday to be my favorite day.

The even more important discovery for me, however, was the way writing could uncover my deeper thoughts, the ones I push down as I go about my day. Stopping to write and reflect slowed me down enough to pay attention to other, perhaps more important thoughts. I had believed in the power of journal writing for a while. This clear demonstration of how my thoughts can be hidden from my conscious thinking gave me still another reason to give students and myself time to think on paper.

As they write, I write. We change our pace, take a deep breath, and get in touch with thoughts that are lingering in our minds, waiting to be revealed. With time to reconsider, look back, and reflect about our learning and our lives, we increase our understanding of who we are, what we know, and what we hope to accomplish.

The writing can take a variety of forms. It may be stream of consciousness, narrative, jottings, a diagram, a cartoon, webs, graphic organizers, an opinion, a letter, a flowchart, or just an assortment of phrases and ideas. There are no right or wrong ways to think on paper. The important piece is that time is taken to pause and capture thoughts. The writing may be reflective, evaluative, questioning, poetic, rambling, incomplete, or a wide range of possibilities.

When students are given time to think about their learning, they discover what it means to them. They personalize it. The content covered is more than just required information to parrot back on a test. As students think about their reading and writing, school becomes about more than completing assignments. It becomes a place that satisfies the internal longing to make sense of the world.

MORE THAN WHICH MATERIALS, WHICH PUBLISHER, OR WHICH bandwagon, *the way students connect to the curriculum* predicts the possibility of lifelong joyful literacy. When kids have time for literate lives, the choices intrinsic in them, an enriched environment in which to grow, and opportunities to think and reflect on what their experiences mean, their literacy connections grow like Jack's beanstalk.

9

Nurturing the Relationship Between Students and Literacy

One day while I was on the treadmill, Rudy Crews, the former chancellor of the New York Public Schools, was being interviewed on television. In describing how schools often fail to engage children, he said: "The visceral connection between the children and what they are to learn is never made. This impacts all aspects of learning."

"Right on, Rudy!" I shouted at the TV. "The visceral connection! That's exactly my point about the student's relationship to the curriculum!" He ignored me and went on talking.

Yes! I thought. Educators know this is a vital chapter in the learning story of each child. The challenge is how we do it. This chapter discusses suggestions that have worked in my classroom and the classrooms of colleagues. They are ways that enrich the connection between students and their reading and writing, the visceral connection that is the heart of all learning. Students who feel they are outside the curriculum have a very different relationship to it than those who feel like insiders. These are the children who feel like they belong, they have a voice, their thoughts and ideas contribute to the learning culture. Not only do they feel like insiders in the literacy club, their sense of being literate individuals radiates from the inside out. This is who they are. "I am a reader. I am a writer." These proclamations feel natural and important to them.

For children to develop a long-lasting relationship to reading, what they do each day during reading time must add to their knowledge of what good readers do when they read. It must be engaging and purposeful. If learning to read isn't pleasurable, books and reading lose their attraction and are discarded as too taxing. When reading and books activate children's imagination and sense of adventure, and stimulates thinking about wonderful ideas, it motivates their commitment to being a reader. The reading strands that follow are common practice in many reading and writing classrooms. As you revisit them here, please consider the important role they play in connecting children to literacy for the long haul.

READING

What Is Reading?

Early in the school year I show students a passage in French that I've copied onto chart paper. With my embarrassing mid-western French accent I carefully read each line. The children look at me totally confused. What had I just read?

Well, I don't know what I read but I could read every word. We talk about what it means to read. Is it pronouncing each word correctly? No. I could pronounce each word in French and still not have a clue what it meant. Did I get any images in my mind while I read? Impossible. Could I make connections to what I already know? No way. Could I predict what was going to happen? Absolutely not. I could only say the words. I couldn't really think about what they meant. Could I ask questions as I read? No. If I don't understand what I'm reading I can't ask questions.

Reading is more than the words on the page. Just reciting the words doesn't allow for meaning making. Reading is thinking. In order to make sense of print readers need to be thinking about the words at the same time they are decoding them. The words on the page are activated in the minds of the readers.

A refrigerator keeps food cold all the time. You don't have to push any buttons just put your milk on the shelf and it will stay cold. The oven is a different matter. You can let your cookie dough sit in the oven all day on the baking sheet and it'll never become cookies. First you have to turn on the oven. Without flipping the switch, the cookies will never bake.

Reading is like the oven. You have to flip the thinking switch in your mind for the words on the page to work. Reading in French for me is like putting cookie dough in a cold oven. It doesn't make sense. A deeper level of thought needs to parallel the decoding for the book to come to life. If children assume reading is passive, they'll never realize its magic in their own lives.

Read Aloud

The literacy club boasts a complete roster of members during read aloud. No one is excluded. No matter their reading level, everyone can relax and listen to an enchanting tale. It doesn't demand expensive curriculum materials, only a worthy book and an audience of eager listeners. And studies show that it is one of the best ways to support young readers (Moustafa 1997). It's a daily reminder for children that reading brings energy and pleasure, and even in the busy schedule of school, a fabulous book makes time stand still for a little while. For some children, it's the time during the school day when they feel most connected to the power of reading. It's a time I feel our relationships to literacy and to each other growing. Our hearts open to the characters as we share their hopes, their dilemmas, and their dreams. These shared moments of emotion and wonder build stronger personal relationships to books and classmates.

The read aloud time after recess is only one of several times I read aloud each day. That's the time I choose a chapter book and model how to read a longer book for maximum pleasure. I usually select books a little beyond the reading level that most children can handle on their own. Listening to more difficult and demanding texts helps prepare kids for reading more challenging books on their own.

Read aloud time is not a luxury in a busy day that can be eliminated in a time crunch. Not only is its value supported by research, but there are many reading and writing lessons embedded in the read aloud time. Here are some that I return to again and again:

- Glance back at the previous chapter to remind myself what I read yesterday.
- Use the title of the chapter to help predict what might happen next.
- At the end of each chapter or section, recall vivid images.
- Talk with others about what has happened so far for additional reminders.
- Reread parts that aren't clear or that I don't understand.
- Use context clues to figure out new or strange words.
- Read dialogue with expression and match voice to character.
- Vary my speed as a reader depending on what's happening in the story.
- Notice the way the author starts and ends chapters.
- Notice use of dialogue.
- Notice character development.

When I read a chapter book after lunch recess, the children may sit anywhere in the room where I can see them and where they can be a good listener. Some children prefer to stretch out on the rug, some like to stay at their seats, and some like to sit next to a friend. I also invite them to finger-knit or draw if they want to. I have found that children can listen very closely to a book and still be quietly drawing a picture or design. My only two requests are that they not walk around or talk. The no talking rule is obvious. The no walking rule is because it makes it harder for me to concentrate on the words if I am distracted by movement. My eyes tend to glance toward the movement and I lose my place. The children use recycled paper for their drawings. Their drawings are usually spontaneous and they don't seem to mind using paper that has print on one side.

Read aloud is a time to broaden the reading repertoire of children. I try to choose among a variety of kinds of books, such as biographies, historical fiction, science fiction, fantasy, realistic fiction, and so on. Children will often try a new genre after they have fallen in love with it during read aloud. It continues to amaze me that so many children want to read a book on their own after they've heard it read aloud.

Reading aloud from a chapter book is one kind of read aloud. I start the reading time in the morning with a picture book. Gathering the children back on the rug, reading the words and showing the illustrations of a fine picture book seems a relaxing and focused way to start our conversations about books. When we do an author's study, I read a book by the featured author or illustrator. If we are studying a genre, theme, poetry, or fairy tales, the picture book follows suit. This is another time for children to fall in love with books.

After I read the book, the children move into a circle to talk about what they noticed or found of interest. Sometimes I ask them to listen with a particular focus in mind. Often, the conversation follows the thinking of the children. My favorite conversations happen when the children do not agree about a book, perhaps its merits or the qualities of the characters. When I read *Next Year I'll Be Special* by Patricia Reilly Giff, most of the class felt Maggie was looking forward to second grade and imagining herself as the star. Maggie's attitude really bothered Justin. He thought she was bragging. A lively discussion ensued and the book was passed back and forth in the circle as children found places in the text that supported their opinion. It was also an excellent lesson in how to disagree without being disagreeable and to emphasize that consensus, while a goal of class meetings, is not a prerequisite of book conversations.

As the volume of books read together grows, our shared literary history grows as well. More and more conversations include children sharing: "That reminds me of the book. . . ." References to previous books knit the community of readers closer together and nourishes their relationship to the curriculum.

Sustained Silent Reading (SSR)

For well over twenty years, read aloud and SSR have been credited as the two most powerful reading activities for helping students grow as readers. Whether we call it SSR, Drop Everything and Read (DEAR) time, or Sustained Quiet Uninterrupted Independent Reading Time (SQUIRT), this sacrosanct time each day is like a daily "reading vitamin" requirement. Although it has been talked about for years, SSR is often deleted when curriculum demands crowd the day. I want to emphasize its important role in connecting students to meaningful reading.

Reasons for Sustained Silent Reading. Recent meetings and conversations with teachers have made me realize that not all teachers manage to find the time for SSR on a regular basis. To me it's a necessity for students if they are to make reading their own. Independent reading strengthens their relationship to reading as they find the right book and get lost in another place and time. There have been times in the hectic day when it seemed more productive to bypass silent reading and move on to more pressing issues, but I knew SSR only looked like a time of quiet with little happening. As I watched students reading independently, I made a list of important components built into this time.

1. There are days when its most important attribute is the silence that falls on the room. Children retreat inside their heads to read and take a respite from the usual demands of the classroom.

2. Students have an opportunity to practice the skills and strategies they are learning.

3. Peer pressure is a positive force. A setting where everyone is reading pulls reluctant readers toward that norm.

4. Book selection, the number one skill of a reader, gets attention and support.

5. Students make recommendations to each other and influence each other to keep reading.

6. Their reading preferences become public and a part of the classroom culture.

7. The reading habit seeps into their bones.

8. Talking with a partner about a book paves the way for being part of a larger book discussion.

Teachers can put this valuable time to good use in several ways:

1. modeling literate behavior by reading silently with students
2. walking quietly among the readers doing a status of the class, jotting down what each child is reading
3. building an awareness of the reading preferences and habits of the students
4. listening to students read short passages to ascertain if the book is appropriate and to listen for signs of progress
5. pulling back and observing students as they read for assessment purposes
6. doing a quick Running Reading Record of a student or two

I make my decision about which of the above to do in an ad hoc way, depending on my sense of the class that day. If Matthew is struggling to read during the allotted time, I may help him get into a book by reading a few pages to him. Personal attention and support go a long way toward helping a child feel more committed to a book.

Book Selection. For children to make a personal connection to reading, they must be able to choose books they can read and that they want to read. SSR is the perfect time to reinforce the number one requirement of any reader: the ability to choose the right book. What more important decision does any reader make? If children learn how to choose a book they will enjoy or use competently, they are on the road to loving books and reading on their own. The right book at the right time is a gift of major proportions. Minilessons and discussions about book selection spiral throughout the year and guide children in their search for the right match. Telling children of my own process gives them additional understanding and awareness of how experienced readers still need to make appropriate and careful choices. Reading is premeditated, not a random act, unless we're in the dentist's or doctor's office. Children who only read assignments miss this vital ingredient in the reading mix. Readers choose books they want to read. SSR is a time we all practice finding the just-right book.

I start the initial discussion about book selection—which goes on for a number of days—by asking students to jot down what they think about when they choose a book. Next I ask one or two children to volunteer to do a think aloud that demonstrates what they think in their heads as they decide whether or not to read a specific book. I bring in three books I plan to read at some point in the future and think aloud about how I choose the one I think will be best for me today. We make a reference chart with their ideas, adding to our list over the course of time. Depending on the students' developmental level, our list will grow to include what aware readers do almost automatically. Choosing a book means investigating:

- the cover
- the blurb on the back
- the size of the print
- print versus white space on pages
- the number of pages
- pictures or illustrations
- number of chapters
- how many pages are in most chapters
- the amount of dialogue and/or description
- length of sentences

Students learn to check these features as they do a quick tour through the book deciding if the level looks appropriate and the topic appealing. Then they read a passage to see if they know most of the words and can read with fluency. If there are more than a few words on a page that are unknown, the text will be too demanding and comprehension will be poor. Research suggests that a 90 percent accuracy rate allows readers to focus on meaning, creating images, and think beyond the words on the page (Pinnell and Fountas 1998, 6). As we teach children how to think as they read, we need to be sure that the books they select allow them to use prior knowledge and that the vocabulary is easy enough so that they can think while they read. When the text is too difficult, thinking goes into deciphering the words and not into comprehension.

Some adult readers feel bound to finishing a book once they've begun. Their strong sense of loyalty to a book dictates they read every page. I don't subscribe to that attitude for myself and especially for young readers. Their memory is too short. If Jason plugs through one book after another without a sense of real engagement, a wonderful book may get him back on the reading track for a while, but once he is home, there are too many other choices for him. If reading feels like a job, something to get through, it will be low on his list, if it makes his list at all.

I've heard teachers worry that if a child is permitted to abandon books, this will become a habit. I think it's an indicator that the child is not yet hooked on reading and isn't making the right book selections. Here's where our expertise comes into play as we guide Jason to books that pull him in and hold him captive.

Talking Partners. Chatting about a book after SSR is another opportunity for children to grow ties to their reading. This talking time is short, no more than three or four minutes, but it gives them an opportunity to process what they read and to listen to how another reader thinks. Before we begin talking with partners, we meet in a circle and two readers demonstrate a good book conversation for the rest of the class. We observe with notebooks in hand and jot down what we notice. The partners share how they thought it went and then we discuss our notes. Why did their conversation work? What might they do differently next time? We make a reference chart of what partners can talk about. These demonstrations take time but make the expectations for this brief talking time explicit. Students learn what it means to talk with a partner about a book, to be an attentive listener, to take turns, and so on—the skills needed in many social settings. Talking about books reinforces their association with their chosen books.

Reading Logs. Reading logs, where students keep track of books they read— and, for older graders, to jot down three to five sentences about what they read—provides a record of their reading habits. As they gain an awareness of their reading preferences, they begin to establish their reader identity. This paves the way for a lifelong relationship with reading.

Every few months I ask kids to go back through their reading log, read their entries, and notice the book choices they have made. What did they learn about their reading habits?

"I noticed I read a chapter book and when I finish it, I read easy books for a few days," said Melissa.

"I've only read the Oz books since January," said Ben. "But I'm not tired of them. I think one of my habits is to read everything by an author."

Jake raised his hand tentatively. "Well, I seem to start two or three books before I find one I like well enough to read it all the way through. I guess that's maybe a habit."

At other times I'll ask students to reread their logs and think about how they've changed and grown as a reader. SSR, when students are choosing their own books and reading independently, gives an accurate overview of reading progress and gives their literacy connections time to grow.

"Where Were You?" Occasionally if we need a change of pace, SSR ends with another activity my colleague Anne Nesbitt shared with me. After the timer

rings, I pose the question, "Where were you? I was just in London riding in a taxi." Hands go up and we spend the next minute or two reveling in all the places we have gone without leaving our room. "I was at Hogwarts," says Joseph. "I was in outer space," says Zach. "I was in a boat at sea," says Carrie. Another time I may ask, "Who were you with?" or "What were you doing?" Their responses to these questions knit our learning community back together after we have traveled so far from each other. These few minutes of unifying closure also highlight the most magical part of reading: the power and possibilities that reside in our imaginations.

Popcorn Reading. Once a month, usually on the first Friday, we celebrate our literacy with Popcorn Reading. It's as simple as it sounds. I pop four or five bags of microwave popcorn, divide them into twenty-four coffee filters (the perfect size and inexpensive if bought in bulk) and with the help of a student or two distribute them to the readers. This uncomplicated monthly ritual brings delight and contentment. No, books don't get greasy. Kids don't beg for more. The routine is well-established and we all relax and savor the crunchy popcorn and the books we choose to read. One February, Dana was upset because her family was leaving for Disney World on Thursday. She would miss popcorn reading on Friday.

Like an elastic band, SSR is stretchable. It can expand to incorporate facets of a sound reading program, such as book talk and quickwrites about books, or it can shrink to simply a quiet time with a book. However it is incorporated into the school day, time to read nourishes the children's relationship to the curriculum. It's what all the instruction and conversations are about—the times when we pick up a just-right book and get blissfully absorbed.

An Author or Genre Study

Organizing reading around an author or genre study within the workshop format allows children to learn in a fluid yet bounded way. They read a number of books of their choice and talk with other readers who are immersed in the same study. There are opportunities for thinking about the topic over a number of weeks and creating a project or representation of what they have learned. Pauses to reflect are built in along the way so children can synthesize and make meaning of what they've been reading and discussing. There are more possibilities for meeting the needs and styles of diverse learners than in a traditional reading setting. As children find links between and among books during a study and make connections to their own lives, their literacy world enlarges.

A well-orchestrated study contains important components of a balanced literacy program. Children have the opportunity to

- hear, read, and talk about fine literature
- make decisions about which books to read
- respond to what they read through drawing and writing
- read the same text through different lenses, revisit it, and talk about the craft of the writer/illustrator
- evaluate books and substantiate their opinions
- think creatively to represent what they have learned
- strengthen their sense of community as they read, write, draw, and construct knowledge together around a common topic
- participate in shared reading, guided reading, independent reading, and read aloud
- focus on the craft of the author/illustrator, which supports their growth as writers

Evaluating What They Read. I list all the titles I can find for the study on a grid so children can rate each book (see pages 134 and 135). I originally gave students a blank grid and asked them to fill in the title as they read a book. The concrete list with the titles typed in makes it easier for children to keep track of their progress and to plan which books they want to read. A few blank spaces at the bottom allows them to add other titles. We rate books on a scale of one to four with the best score a four. Reading partners talk with each other about their ratings but do not have to agree. Some young fans decide every book an author writes deserves a four. As readers become more discriminating they differentiate more in their ratings. Whether students rate books as accurately as I might wish, the conversation about the ratings enlivens the reading context.

"What do you think?" is an empowering question and shifts the student's relationship to literacy from passive to active. Asking children their opinions and impressions of a book delivers the message, "You're a reader. Your thoughts matter." And of course, that's the goal—to get students to think about books, to revisit them, to examine them closely, and to decide for themselves what rating the books deserve.

Group share and peer conferring accomplish the same objective. Implicit in the question "What do you feel, see, hear, and connect to in the writing?" is the underlying premise: You're a writer. You know what fine writing sounds like. What do you think? When children pause to think again about text—whether in books, anthologies, or student-generated writing—it asks them to think like a writer, feel like a writer, play the role of a writer. Gradually the *role* of the writer disappears and the child grows into an aware author.

After a kindergarten child reads her story to the class, hands fly into the air. Children want to give their opinion—to have their voice heard. They feel like they have more stature in the group as they offer their ideas. They are writers helping one another. When students evaluate text from the point of view of someone who crafts their own writing, it places them in a position of authority and changes their relationship to the text.

Below is a reference chart developed by my second graders about halfway through the school year. Each year the rubric is worded differently but says similar things. It is important, however, that each class create their own rating rubric. A rating scale from a previous class feels like wearing a pair of borrowed sneakers. The process of developing the rubric is as worthwhile as the rubric itself. It offers an excellent opportunity to talk about what makes a good book and invites everyone to belong to the literacy club as they offer ideas. It is also a useful guide to refer to during writing workshop.

HOW WE RATE BOOKS

A four book:
Makes you wonder
Makes sense—you can understand it
Is the right reading level
Has kind people
Is interesting—you can get into the story
Is exciting and adventurous
Is properly written and edited
Is one you would buy
Is one of which you never tire

A three book:
Is a good book
Is one you like medium
Is one you don't understand that well
Has some things missing
Is plain and sometimes boring

A two book:
Is a little lame

Is one you don't like
Is one where you don't get it — it's confusing
Leaves you feeling like you want to give up
Is OK but not OK

A one book:
Begins and goes nowhere
Is bad, horrible, and you hate it
Has no middle and no problem
Puts you to sleep
Has writing that doesn't match the pictures in your head
Doesn't make sense
Is hard to understand

Immersion and Partner Reading. The first few days of a new author or genre study brings renewed energy to the class. The fresh collection of books and the anticipation of new learning recharges us. I do a soft sell as I read the first book aloud. I hope the children will appreciate and enjoy the author's work or genre as much as I do. After we talk about the book in our learning circle and I assign partners (perhaps with their previous input), students spread out in the room to sample books. Like choosing chocolate from a box of Godiva, some grab a tasty-looking one and others spend more time, determined to make the best choice.

Reading with a partner and talking about the illustrations and story add more thinking and awareness. I circulate among the partners, listening in, asking questions about their process, and measuring their engagement.

Hilary and George decide to take turns reading every other page aloud. Walt and Tommy read silently and talk after they've read two pages. Cynthia reads aloud to Richard while he studies the illustrations. He'll have his turn to read later in the book. Reading and book talk fills the room. *Yes!* I think. *This is productive! This is fun!*

Partner reading takes patient modeling and coaching, but it pays important dividends. It builds a strong sense of community as children learn how to work thoughtfully and well with each other. It also provides support for readers as they read the text and process what they've read. As I skim around the room listening in and rooting out teachable moments, I have half as many stops when the students are working with a partner. Classrooms feel more relaxed and on task when children clearly know they are expected to work cooperatively with each other.

Reading Response Sheets. In addition to reading, reading, reading, and rating the books, students are expected to do a response sheet (with a picture space and lines for writing) or reading journal entry, depending on the grade level. The number of responses varies from child to child but they are not expected to write about each book they read. I would rather have a larger portion of their time going to actual reading.

Students do not have to answer questions after each book they read to prove that they have read it. Completing a worksheet with comprehension questions teaches very little except perseverance. It changes getting immersed in the author's books from a stroll down a country lane to a hurdle event. When a follow-up worksheet is attached to a book like a barnacle to a boat, it deters young readers from the excitement of exploration.

For many years I did comprehension questions automatically, following the pattern in basals and workbooks. Five eager second-grade readers helped me learn the downside of those questions. They were excited to learn more about Helen Keller, who had once lived in our town. Before I brought in copies of her biography, I combed through each chapter for vital information and vocabulary words and made questions for students to answer. After four chapters of reading and answering questions, I had squelched their desire to read the book. The children dragged through our discussions and found the questions unimportant and tedious. My focus pulled their reading off-track. They explained they could no longer read the story. Now they were reading to find answers. I shuddered. In my zest to squeeze the most out of the book, I had drained it of all relevance and pleasure. The next day children brought their own questions and concerns about what they had read to our conversation.

Unlike comprehension questions, response sheets invite children to find their own meaning in books. They reinforce the expectation that readers make personal connections to texts. When kids find personal meaning in what they read, it's another step toward long-term literacy.

As Katherine Paterson says, "It is the privilege of the reader to discover what a book means for his or her particular life. The book either speaks for itself to the reader or it fails to speak" (1989, 15). Too many times as a reading teacher I had treated a book like a puppy, trying to make it sit up and speak to reluctant readers through questions, vocabulary lists, and chapter reviews. Teachers and students have helped me learn to trust the books and to take my cue from readers.

Turning kids loose to read without specific comprehension questions feels like turning them loose in the Museum of Natural History. Will they get lost? Will they spend their time wisely? What if they miss the dinosaur exhibit on the fourth floor? Letting them roam takes courage and confidence—in kids, in books, and in our own teaching practices. Guided reading, individual conferences, and class discussions tell me what I need to know about how students are reading. I don't have to check comprehension of each book with a list of questions that bog children down and leave them with less time and desire to read.

Writing About Books. Talking about books in our learning circle is a precursor for writing about them. Our conversations give students ideas for what they can write on their response sheets. Sometimes the focus of response sheets is assigned for a few days as children learn how to write about character, setting, problem, solution, and so forth. As they become comfortable writing about the different literary elements, they can choose which one to use. At other times, the focus may be a comprehension strategy, such as accessing prior knowledge, and children write about the connections they make to the book.

Our reference chart about "What We Can Write About Books" grows along with the children's awareness of possibilities. Here is a list from a second-grade class:

WHAT WE CAN WRITE ABOUT BOOKS

characters

setting

problem and solution

This book reminds me of . . .

This story needed more . . .

The story is like . . .

What I think is special about this story is . . .

The problem in/with the story is . . .

My favorite character in this story is . . .

Some words I really liked in the story are . . .

This book is like another one I know because . . .

This book makes me think of . . .

What I notice in the book is . . .

keys and locks (things that let you into the book and things that make it hard)

Once students understand each of the ways to respond, they can select the response that seems most appropriate to the book they are reading. Finding their own connection to the book is much more satisfying than answering questions to prove that they read the book. Response sheets deliver the message that each reader is capable of making important observations about the book. This more open-ended response to literature fits neatly within the clear boundaries of an author or genre study, offering students a sense of independence and responsibility.

Sticky Notes and Highlighters.   Sometimes I ask children to read with a particular focus in mind, using sticky notes to mark places to think more about. As an adult reader, the books I read usually sprout sticky notes like a bad hair day. Lines I want to return to are highlighted and I have imaginary talks with the author through notes in the margins. When a child reads a book and marks passages with sticky notes, it's almost like an animal marking his territory. The student's connections to the book are obvious and concrete.

Whenever kids read consumable materials, I make sure they have a highlighter handy. I model how I use one and give them plenty of opportunities to discover how highlighters can help them understand a text better. Sticky notes and highlighters are magic wands that increase student attention to the text. Here are some of the ways teachers have asked students to use them during reading:

PLEASE MARK

- a part you could really see
- where you have a question
- a humorous part
- where the dialogue tells you more about the character
- where the author uses special language—beautifully crafted language
- vocabulary you don't understand
- where you could really feel the story
- a place that helps you predict
- a favorite line
- a part you would like to talk about
- a part that makes you wonder
- a part you don't like
- a very important or exciting part
- a part with tension
- a good part to read aloud

- a part that helps you know the character better
- a part that gives you a clear picture of the setting

Sticky notes and highlighters are authentic aids that experienced readers rely on to help them understand and remember what they read. They add a sense of purpose and seriousness to reading and maneuver students closer to the text. This closer connection improves comprehension and eases children toward lifelong meaning making from print.

Favorite Books. I'm always curious to know which books the children prefer by each author or in the genre that we've studied. My real reason for asking about their favorites is the thoughtful conversation it generates as students explain their decisions. It's another chance for children to create a bond with books.

Second graders loved reading the Arthur books by Marc Brown long before television made them so commercial and popular. After the children had had a number of days to read, write, and talk about the Arthur books, I typed all the titles into a chart of small boxes I made on my computer. I asked children to cut out the boxes and arrange them in order of their preferences with their very favorite title on top. We had a good time comparing the books and talking about why and how they chose the three favorites they put on top.

Evan asked if he could glue the little boxes on construction paper in order of preference. Of course! Several other children followed his wise example. It was so much easier to see and compare favorites when they were glued on bright paper. The next year, I explained the assignment and showed the class both possibilities. Jaclyn came up with her own improved version. She turned the construction paper vertically like a thermometer. She glued her favorite book at the top to show it was the "hottest." It was even easier to look at her finished project and know which books were her favorites. Lital folded her large yellow paper into thirds. She glued the little boxes under these headings: *Love it!, Like it a lot,* and *So-So.* Each year the rating activity is enriched by the ideas of students. When I am open to their influence and ideas, it refines the work we do together and sends a message to the students that I value their creativity. Their relationship to the curriculum becomes more resilient when they are helping to shape it.

Time to Make Learning Permanent. Projects bring out the more creative and imaginative side in students. For the kinesthetic learner, this hands-on time is a welcome invitation into the literacy club. The end of an author's study is a great time to rev up the energy as children create representations of their learning. Sometimes we have done more structured group efforts, like a mural or reader's theatre. Other times children have decided how to represent their learning and whether to work alone or in a group.

Reader's Theatre.   Reader's theatre is a fun way for children to make books come alive. When the class finished the entertaining books by James Marshall, a play about his winsome character Fox seemed like a natural extension. Not one for elaborate productions at the end of September, I opted for reader's theatre. With reader's theatre, every word and line of the text is part of the performance. It's like a group reading a story. Sometimes several students read the same lines to vary the sounds. Parts aren't memorized, but read with dramatic flair. Performers sit or stand in one place and read their parts. Imagine a whole family reading a bedtime story aloud.

I typed up each of the five chapters in *Fox on the Job* exactly as James Marshall had written them. I divided the class into five groups of five each and we were ready to roll.

I met with each chapter group to assign parts. Students used highlighters to mark their parts as I divided up the lines. I assigned the more unsure readers short but funny parts, such as when Fox says, "Oh, rats!"

Students went off to practice their lines while I met with the next chapter group. With only a couple of quick run-throughs, we were ready. The chapter one group sat in five chairs at the front of the room with their scripts. They read their lines perfectly, but something was missing. Wait a minute! I thought. James Marshall's charming illustrations are half the fun of his books.

That afternoon I made transparencies of several illustrations from each chapter on the copy machine. The next morning students volunteered to color them in with transparency markers. Now we really were ready to roll. *Fox on the Job,* take two!

The chapter one group sat in front of the projection screen. As they read their lines, I changed the transparencies to match. This time we all laughed. The illustrations made the words funny. We performed our little production for two other classes and were proud of how well it went. The third time was one too many, but we got through. The technique, however, is a winner. Reader's theatre accompanied by overhead transparencies is a manageable and surefire way to do a whole class play that children, teacher, and audience all enjoy.

Performing a book gives children a sense that it belongs to them. It will always be a part of them, just as I remember being in "The Three Little Bears" in first grade. The literacy club cannot be limited to reading and writing. It needs to include other avenues for discovering the pleasures of language, such as skits, plays, choral readings, and reader's theatre. For some children, bringing text to life through drama is their entrée into a relationship with literacy.

Individual or Small-Group Projects.   A journal entry I wrote at a Bard College workshop gives a sense of what I mean by a project:

> My third graders had finished reading *Stone Fox* by John Gardiner. They were stunned by the abrupt ending and excited to do a representation from the book. I asked them on Tuesday if they'd like to have a reading time to work on a project and we agreed it would take two days. OK Wednesday and Thursday to work alone or with a partner—Friday for presentations. Wednesday A.M. was I surprised! Elana arrived with a full bag of polyester fluff to use as snow and Lego men for figures. Carrie brought wood and Popsicle sticks. Jason had Styrofoam to build a house, Mei had Playmobile figures and a shoe box. The list goes on. It was as if they'd been waiting for weeks for this invitation. Wednesday at 11:00 they got started. Any supplies I had they were welcome to use: clay, pipe cleaners, construction paper, glue, paints, etc. Ethan and Nick (as unlikely a team as the Odd Couple) sat side by side at two computers writing the sequel to the book, talking through ideas then writing the same text. Max and Mei, another totally unexpected team, shaped clay into sled dogs. Katrina, Elana, and Carrie glued wood together back in the corner, chatting and planning. As I walked around asking how it was going, I really didn't have to ask. They were talking about the details of the book and how they could represent it in their project. Charles and Zach finished their clay pieces and offered to help Jason and Michael. Alex worked alone, totally absorbed. Watching them made me feel proud and guilty. Why haven't we done more of this? They were so alive! Their standards were high along with their commitment.

A positive energy entered the room along with the polyester fluff and Styrofoam. This opportunity to create and express themselves brought a fervor and joy. The hard work felt productive. Please don't think I had never let the class have more than pencils and lined paper up to this point—there had been other projects, but the students obviously longed for more. When given the time, some precious creative force is unleashed in children and brings out the best in them. Sometimes I think fear of classroom chaos limits how often I turn kids loose to work on projects. I forget that these are the times they are most on task, because it is their task.

As teachers plan a balanced literacy program, time for projects must be included. With the overemphasis on state test scores and other pressures to cover the curriculum, time for active, industrious learning can get relegated to the later that never comes. Children are more invested in reading when given time to represent and hold on to their learning. Working on projects during class time (not as a homework assignment that frustrates Dad or Mom) makes students feel more connected to what they've read and to their classmates. Relationships are revitalized.

I have talked about an author or genre study in detail because they contain the essential elements in a sound reading program and are a prototype for other studies. The various parts adapt smoothly for a nonfiction study such as bats, a genre study such as poetry, or a theme study such as friendship. Immersion, focused study, and project/share offer opportunities for readers to create their own crucial links to the topic. When everyone in the class is involved in the same broad study regardless of reading level, the reading hierarchy flattens. Everyone reads books by the author and takes part in discussions about his style. Guided reading groups give the teacher time to support more uncertain readers as they read the author's books at their level. Author and genre studies welcome everyone into the literacy club.

I have taught reading in a number of ways in my long history as a teacher. As the building reading teacher for seven years back in the 1970s, I worked with children who found it difficult to learn to read. Then I trusted the skills in the basal workbook to be all they needed to get over the reading hurdle. I would teach them differently now. We have learned the importance of feeling successful when learning to read. We know we have to take our cue from children and teach them what they are ready to learn. And we must be sensitive to the relationships they are establishing to reading. Are they enthusiastic? Is there a solid learning curve? Do they initiate reading and talk to classmates about books they really liked? Thoughtful and adaptive teachers are alert to the signals kids transmit about their reading and change course if a healthy relationship isn't developing. Teaching children to read needs to be replaced by teaching children to be aware readers who choose to read. This, of course, depends on the relationship we foster between children and their reading.

WRITING

I enjoy writing, but I am not so naïve as to think all children and adults share my pleasure. What makes writing so hard for so many? Important classroom research over the past two decades guides us in answering that question. We know *it's hard to care about writing*

- when it's an assignment read and judged solely by the teacher
- when we haven't discovered writing's transformational power in our lives

- when we worry we won't have the right words to say what we intend
- when we don't know that first drafts can be far from perfect
- when we don't know how to revise our writing to make it better
- when we don't have time for writing we care about
- when our teacher teaches from a distance—and never gets her swimsuit wet
- when our teacher doesn't understand the complexities of writing
- when our teacher doesn't know us well enough to give us helpful guidance

Like many things in life, it's easier to know what *not* to do than to know exactly what to do. But research and experience translate *what makes writing hard* into how to help children connect to writing in a way that sticks.

Writing in my classroom has two parts: writing workshop, at least four times a week, when children participate in full-fledged authoring, and the journal entries, letters, notes, and so on that they write at other times during the week. All of these writing experiences contribute to a child's sense of being a writer. Their frequency and clear expectations help students to feel that writing is within their comfort zone—a necessity if they are to establish a long-term writing relationship.

Making Explicit the Transformational Nature of Writing

Spotlighting the transformational nature of writing is one way to hook children on its value. When our writing taps into a rich vein of thinking we didn't know was there, the surprise whets the appetite for more discoveries.

Just as readers are pulled into a book to find out what's going to happen, young writers can experience the magic of having their stories emerge from the unknown. A third grader, Suzanne, explained this idea to me:

> When I read, I don't know what's going to happen, so I want to keep reading. When I write a story, I don't know what's going to happen either. I never know what's going to pop into my mind. That's what makes me want to write.

Putting words on paper tweaks Suzanne's sense of adventure. She becomes an explorer of her own unknown territory. For students to grasp her astute awareness, they need frequent and regular times to write about topics important to them. They need repeated experiences of exploration and discovery to trust it will continue to happen. And they need to appreciate and celebrate this special feature of writing.

At the end of writing workshop or when children have done other writing, I reinforce this transformational feature of writing with one of the following questions: "Who wrote something today that surprised you?" "Who wrote something you didn't even know you knew?" "Who wrote something they never would have predicted they would write today?" When our thinking changes in the process of writing, or we clarify our thinking as we write, or we unearth a thought that had been deeply buried by the rush of the day our energy changes. Writing brings a little jolt of adrenaline and pleasure. These little jolts over time add up to a live circuit between the child and writing. Suzanne doesn't need a teacher to plug her in when it's time to write.

Distance

Writing changes with time, or rather, my opinion about my writing does. When I finish a piece of writing and I've crafted it to the best of my ability, it usually pleases me. But letting the piece take a nap for a few weeks in a folder before I read it again gives me the necessary distance to see what works and what doesn't work. Too many times what I read with pride a month earlier has transformed in the file like bread collecting mold. Yikes! Time lets me read my writing as if someone else had written it. My close attachment has waned and necessary revisions are glaring. My stance switches from author to editor. Writing is recursive and I make revisions even as I draft. But for me to be truly satisfied with my writing, I need the distance of time.

Children experience this same phenomenon. Kat wrote about a family ski weekend in January. In April she decided she would like to type her story on the computer to publish. As she typed, she was surprised at the details she had left out.

"I can't believe it," she told me. "I didn't say where we went or how nervous I was the first time down the slope." Kat had changed her mind about what she wanted to say, so changing her text was easy.

Jennifer, a second grader, reread her story "The Bluebird" after several months. "Oh! I hate this ending!" she complained. "What was I thinking?"

I had to agree with her. She had grown as a writer in the intervening months. Now she could imagine a much more appropriate resolution to her story.

Too often we ask children to make revisions—change their text—before they're distanced enough to have changed their minds. Then the process of revision feels unnatural and not something they are ready to do. Returning to a piece of writing after a few weeks gives children a fresh perspective. School schedules don't always allow time for writing to ripen in a folder, but every once in a while it is helpful if children can learn firsthand the advantage of going back to their writing after some time has elapsed. Ways to improve the text will be more obvious and students can celebrate their growth as a writer.

Creating a Collection

My response group for the Artists-Writers Workshop elected to read *Art and Fear: Observations on the Perils (and Rewards) of ARTMAKING* (Bayles and Orland 1993). When the book arrived in my mailbox I opened it to check out the print size, readability, and other qualities that meant I could read it in time for the next class. The book fell open to page twenty-nine. I skimmed down the page and broke into a smile.

The authors tell the story of a ceramics teacher who divided his class into two groups. Half the class was graded on the quality of their best pot. The other half was graded on the quantity, determined by weight, of the work completed during the course.

> Well, came grading time and a curious fact emerged: the works of highest quality were all produced by the group being graded for quantity. It seems that while the "quantity" group was busily churning out piles of work—and learning from their mistakes—the "quality" group had sat theorizing about perfection, and in the end had little more to show for their efforts than grandiose theories and a pile of dead clay. (Bayles and Orland 29)

A goal of perfection in writing limits output and growth. Students need continuous opportunities to write in a variety of genres and for a variety of purposes and for a variety of audiences. Creating a collection of writing over time gives students the experiences necessary to develop fluency and to use their growing body of knowledge about the craft of writing. The collection may contain:

- journal or notebook entries
- weekend news
- writing in math, social studies, and science
- letters to the teacher and classmates
- letters home to parents on Friday
- narratives, poems, expository writing, and other genres from reading and writing workshop

Younger writers are impressed with length and volume. Asked to choose their best piece, a first or second grader will inevitably say it's the longest one, unless it's the story about their birthday. It's as if they know that more words written means more practice and more growth. The environment for writing needs to be supportive of trial and error and patient with less than perfection. Teaching children about the writing process and rough drafts grants them permission to create a lopsided pot. The next one may or may not be better, but repeated attempts will gradually show improvement. A classroom that honors honest effort and accepts mistakes as opportunities to learn makes this possible. The habits of writers will refuse to take root if the environment is not supportive, intimate, and accepting and the student's relationship to writing remains fragile and tentative.

Fine Literature as Textbooks

Fine literature is another required source of continual nourishment for young writers. I used to think that the reading/writing connection was writing about the book, such as book reports or story starters. Then I started to write my own childhood memories. Suddenly I wanted them to sound like the stories of real writers, like Barbara Kingsolver or Mary Gordon. My own desire to write led me to look more closely at the craft of writers. Books by admired authors became my textbooks; fine writing held lessons I wanted to learn and share with students.

"Illuminating the craft of the writer,"—words I first heard from a writing teacher—are the heart of the reading/writing connection. I wrapped the phrase in a small white hankie, just as I did my milk money many years ago, and tucked it safely in the back of my mind. Since then, my experience as a writer and teacher has given that phrase shape and definition. When children view a published book as writing by another author, they add a deeper dimension to the act of reading: learning about writing. As teachers illuminate the craft of the writer during reading, children take note and begin to notice and appreciate well-crafted writing.

Teaching the Tools

Children who understand that they can go back to a story and write a new lead are less anxious about getting started. Experiencing the writing process, not as a lock-step plan that everyone does together like the Rockettes, but as a recursive process that allows writers to improve text at any point as it unfolds, gives students permission to write drafts that are rough thoughts on paper.

Students deserve to learn the tools of the writing craft. When they know there are options for improving as writers—use stronger verbs, include specific and important details, and so on, writing doesn't feel so insurmountable. This, of course, means we must teach them. Several books by Ralph Fletcher are my favorite guides as I teach writing. *What a Writer Needs* (1993),

A Writer's Notebook: Unlocking the Writer Within You (1996), and *Live Writing: Breathing Life into Your Words* (1999) give excellent advice about what young writers need to know. Listening carefully to students and continually assessing their writing to see what they are ready to learn is another key to knowing what to teach.

An accomplished writer knows that language is flexible and can be crafted. When emergent writers first write a few letters to describe their drawing, the effort of writing precludes the willingness to revise. It's as though they've carried all the household furniture up three flights of stairs—please don't tell them they have moved it to the wrong apartment. But as young writers become fluent and can transcribe their thoughts with more ease, they need to know that words are like gymnasts: they can do back flips, splits, vault over hurdles, and leap in the air and land on a narrow beam. By rearranging words, meaning changes. By rearranging sentences, ideas are clarified. By choosing strong verbs and visual nouns, readers can create a better picture in their imaginations. Teachers must teach the tools that allow writers to feel more like a language gymnast and less like the Tin Man.

Some children just intuitively know how to make their writing come alive. Perhaps it's all the reading they do or maybe it's a natural propensity with words. These children are like the pace car in an auto race. Their writing will often signal what other writers may be ready to learn. When Michael exploded the moment in a story, I knew other children would be ready to hear about that writing strategy. When Samantha had her characters talk, I knew there would be others ready to learn about dialogue. The foundation for teaching all the writing tools is the fine literature that children are reading every day. Noticing how another author writes a fabulous lead or chooses short sentences to build tension gives students concrete examples of how it's done. Watching their teacher compose and offering their ideas helps children understand that words on paper on not carved in stone.

Children need to know what they do in their writing that works. Ben, a new student from England, reminded me of this lesson when I was first working in a writing workshop format. He had written a delightful story about a rat that lived in a drainpipe. The only problem was that his spelling was so impossible to read that a teacher who focused on surface errors would miss the imagination and creativity. It was the perfect example to use at an afternoon workshop for teachers. I asked Ben if I could borrow his story to make a copy. He agreed with pride.

When I returned his story to him, Ben asked in his charming British accent, "Please, Mrs. Skolnick, would you tell me what I did right so I can do it again?" Yes, Ben. Absolutely! Of course I must tell you and all young writers what they're doing right. As I teach the tools that writers use, I give children the vocabulary for talking about their writing. They know what it means to extend a sentence, to explode the moment, to give vivid details. Charts on the wall remind them of what makes writing work for the reader and their ideas have contributed to the lists. We have a shared vocabulary and understanding so we can talk about what they are doing right and what goals they can set for themselves.

One thing I've learned as a writer is that writing ain't easy. Most of the time I enjoy it, but there are times I feel like I'm trying to recite the Gettysburg Address in French. I don't have any of the words I need. Then there's the problem of organization, spelling, punctuation, and audience—good grief! Does it really matter to anyone else that I'm writing this?

Teachers bring a reverence and respect to the teaching of writing when they have wrestled with words and felt that frustration. When Julie can't decide what to write about, my empathy and encouragement are sincere. I know that feeling and I also know it's not permanent. It's just very real when it hits. Together we'll solve this temporary glitch.

Teaching the tools that writers use to craft language and demonstrating how those tools create a flexibility of language contribute to the students' growing sense that they can do this, too. In an environment where everyone is apprenticing the same craft, children find their work with words and ideas less burdensome. It's a shared endeavor. As children's knowledge about writing expands, so does their connection to it. They discover ways writing can be effective and yet personalized. This lengthy and purposeful developmental progression requires a relationship to writing that is experimental and motivated by a desire to improve. It is our job to teach students the strategies that make improving a welcome challenge.

Drawing

When my son, Scott, was four years old, he walked into the kitchen holding a picture he had made. "Look, Mommy," he said proudly. "I drew a story." As he drew his castle with a knight, he imagined a story. Young children know pictures tell stories. Adults tend to pay more attention to the words on a page and relegate illustrations to a secondary role. At least that's how I used to do it in my fourth-grade class of yesteryear. I'd assign another of my winning topics (at least I thought they were winning. I never actually tried to write about them myself to see if they won any prizes) and one or two children would ask if they could draw a picture. "After you finish writing," I'd reply, just like my mother used to tell me—after I finished my dinner I could have dessert.

Drawing is not dessert—it's thinking and communicating. It's a fabulous appetizer or even the main course in some settings. The work of

Dr. Karen Ernst daSilva opened my eyes to the potential in drawing (see Karen's insightful book *Picturing Learning* [1994]). Drawing

- activates the brain as students think about their drawing
- organizes thoughts
- accesses memory and emotions
- uncovers details that might be missed in writing
- slows us down to notice and appreciate

The benefits of drawing go far beyond my quick list, but again, it's a case of having to experience it to believe it. Given permission to work in a mode that best serves them, most students seem to intrinsically understand the value of drawing with writing. Tentative students can make an instantaneous attitude shift when drawing receives the seal of approval.

Drawing or sketching aids writers as they draft any writing: stories, nonfiction pieces, poetry, journal writes, and so forth. When my class read *Shoeshine Girl* by Clyde Robert Bulla, I asked students to bring their observation journals to the learning circle as reading workshop began. I read the first chapter aloud, stopping halfway through. I asked them to sketch something they thought was important from the chapter or something they could clearly imagine. Children stretched out on their stomachs to sketch. I sketched along with them. One requirement in their observation journal is that they write about their drawing, explaining why they drew what they did or their thoughts about it. I treasured the moment as I gazed around the circle. Everyone was stretched out sketching, totally engrossed. (We decided to call this activity "Stretch to Sketch" based on Jerome Harste's "Sketch to Stretch," when readers stretch their thinking by drawing.) We then sat back up in the circle and listened carefully to each other. Students were curious to know what others chose to draw and write from the chapter. We were surprised by the variety of drawings, yet each one made sense.

Sometimes sketching eases children into writing. Sometimes more elaborate pictures with colorful details are the harbinger of the story to come. Respect for the power of drawing and art as a way into writing is gradually receiving recognition in classrooms. Watching Charles absorbed in a watercolor picture may not appear to be the best preparation for the state writing test. However, when his later writing contains thoughtful, descriptive language based on his picture, painting seems worthy of his time. And it is.

Revision, often a least favorite subject for fledgling writers, is less arduous when they enlist the help of art. Last week I visited a class of fifth graders who had been working on a family memory. Many felt their stories were at or near completion. We spent half an hour creating pictures based on their stories. What clear image do you want the reader to have after reading your memory? I asked. Students choose markers, colored pencils, pens, and watercolors to illustrate something from their story. When the music stopped after thirty minutes, students talked with a partner about their process. Did it go well? How did their thinking change as they worked? What new insights did they have about their writing?

After a few minutes to debrief with their partner, students wrote for five minutes about their process and their picture. Many were amazed by how much they had to say as they filled more than one page with their thoughts.

The next day we worked in the computer lab. I asked students to consider what they learned from their artwork and make any revisions in a different color font. As I walked around the room and read over their shoulders or talked with them about their revisions, I was elated. Computer screens displayed colorful fonts of additional detail or dialogue. Drawing or painting had slowed them down to think in images about their stories. The black and white printer printed each story in black and gray, but the changes were easy to spot. Their willingness to think on paper in a different way, with paints and markers, brought new ideas and energy to their writing.

A colleague who teaches second grade reported similar results with her students. Inviting children to draw, paint, or sculpt before they begin their revision process highlights parts of the writing that can be improved. The artistic rendering of a story gently invites writers to re-see their work through a visual lens. Students can initiate their own revisions based on their artwork.

Quickwrites

Quickwrites are not story starters. Children do write to an assigned topic, but it's for a short period of time, three to six minutes depending on the developmental level. The biggest difference between a quickwrite and the old story starter writing prompt is that students may stop what they're writing when the timer rings. They don't have to finish what they've begun unless they choose to do so.

Why assign writing that might go nowhere? Quickwrites help students build fluency as writers. As they pour their thoughts onto paper, they are practicing the habit of jumping in and running with a topic. Thinking on paper and keeping up with thoughts is a challenge, whether at a keyboard or with a pencil. Practice during the year helps those who have trouble getting started. When children practice in short bursts, without the expectation of crafting, they can relax and give it a go. Most are surprised and pleased with their results.

Another reason I take time every couple of weeks for a quickwrite before writing workshop is to broaden the repertoire of the writers in the class. Jonathan likes to write football game play-by-plays. Sophia likes to write about sleepovers and girlfriends. Ethan writes science fiction. Writing briefly to an assigned topic offers the possibility that students will discover other types of stories or genre.

I have found that four or five children choose to stay with their quickwrite and work on it during writing workshop. This makes me realize that when I assign a prompt (four times a year, required to practice for the state mastery test) and children are expected to write a complete piece, only about four or five children find the topic a match.

Quickwrites are just like they sound. Before writing workshop begins, I write several invitations for writing on the board and set the timer for four minutes. Younger children may need more time because of their slower pace. We each decide which topic to try and start writing. The one requirement is that they must keep their pencils moving. When the timer rings, we utter a collective sigh. We did it! We thought on paper for an intense four minutes. Some children hate to stop and some are relieved. If children are excited about what they wrote, we may take a few minutes to hear some of the quickwrites. Once a special needs child asked if she could draw her quickwrite. She did a quickdraw.

The short nature of a quickwrite grants students permission to write their first thoughts and to be satisfied with a very rough, timed draft. Most children are pleasantly surprised at what they spurt out in just a few minutes, yet are grateful to be able to leave it unfinished and imperfect.

Here are a few quickwrite invitations I have used:

- The door opened . . .
- a time you were really mad
- a special place
- a special friend
- a time you were scared
- a time you got the giggles
- a family member
- a family memory
- a vacation memory
- back in time or in the future
- feelings (bored, misunderstood, etc.)
- use a sentence in a story or poem to start

- an idiom
- an animal story
- an inanimate object comes to life

My concern as I write about quickwrites is that they will become an excuse to have children write more often to assigned topics. It's not a quickwrite unless students can leave it after the timer rings. Quickwrites are done with a light attitude that says "Let's see what happens if we all write for four minutes to one of these invitations. When the timer rings you're done, unless, of course, you want to continue." Teacher participation is an absolute must. No exceptions! It changes the feel of quickwrites from a playful challenge to just another assignment when the teacher sits at her desk and reads the staff bulletin while children write. Every positive encounter with writing, even short experimental ones, contributes to the confidence of young writers.

In my district, staff development workshops often include quickwrites. It's a few minutes when teachers quiet their minds and focus on the matters at hand. Quickwrites clear a space so deep and rich conversations can begin.

Coached Writing

Coached writing is a playful way to help students see how specific details give the reader a better visual image. If I am told "Elephants flew by the window," I don't have as clear a picture in my head as I do when I'm told "Five elephants flew by the window." Even such small details as color and number add clarity to the reader's movie-in-the-mind. I've not tried it lower than third grade, but I've modified it to use in weekend news for younger children (see below). Finding examples of clarifying details first in reading makes coached writing more meaningful.

The writing activity starts with children beginning a piece of writing that I assign, much like a quickwrite. I don't do a coached writing when students are drafting their own pieces in writing workshop, as they may be reluctant to make arbitrary changes.

For example, after a snow day, I started a coached writing lesson in a fifth grade this way: "What a surprise! It's a snow day!" I explained that I would be asking them to add details to their story as they composed. I would be writing along with them and every few minutes ask them to embed a specific kind of detail as they continued writing.

Children copied the two short lead sentences (or their choice of opening) and began creating a story about what happened on a snow day. I began my story, too. Two or three minutes into our writing I called out, "Add a color." This is fairly easy for most children to do. They don't have to follow the directions immediately but are to try and add it at some point. I write each request I make on the board. Mary added "red" to: "I put on my (red) mittens." After a few more minutes I said, "Add a number." Steve added "forty" to his sentence: "I made (forty) snowballs."

Details I might ask students to add are:

- color
- number
- sound, something they could hear
- odor or smell
- a feeling
- dialogue
- another character
- a question
- an exclamation
- a movement
- a suspicious object

I usually limit my requests to five or six per writing time. Students who choose may ignore my suggestions. Most try to do it and enjoy the challenge. When we share our stories, even though many are not completed, students hear how the embedded details give clearer images.

Adding the teacher's suggestions during the act of writing is the scaffolding some children need to eventually include details on their own. Older children may be able to handle adding a strong verb, an adjective, an adverb, a prepositional phrase, or another part of speech that makes writing more descriptive and visual. The intent of coached writing is to coach children as they are writing in a way that is exploratory and nonthreatening.

The relaxed atmosphere in the room during the twenty-minute coached writing gives it a game-like feel. We all face the same challenge: fitting an unexpected word into an ongoing story. The social context connects students to students as they juggle words in animated compliance. Surrounded by other children showing concern about adding a word, struggling writers feel a bond to the other writers. Writing feels OK.

With second graders, after several months of writing weekend news I ask them to try to add one of the details from the list in their news. For example, for a few weeks I may ask them to add a color. Then I may ask them to add a number. Adding the detail is an option and my requests depend on the readiness of the group. Most students find ways to include my suggestions. I only do this simplified version of coached writing after we have spent many weeks noticing details in our reading.

The Reading/Writing Connection

Facilitating a strong connection between students and their reading and writing feels so positive and right. I know their relationship to reading and writing is a personal preference and not just school work when:

- Children begin to initiate reading and writing.
- They are eager for someone to talk to about the books they're reading and the stories they're writing.
- They think about their reading and writing all day, not just during those times in school.
- They lose track of time while reading or writing and enter a state of flow.
- They have a strong sense of what they want to read, and writing ideas pop into their heads at random.
- They believe that their thoughts about reading and writing contribute to the literary community in which they spend their days.

This is what I want for all children: a relationship to reading and writing that starts in the heart, moves to the mind, and extends out into the world. It's not a relationship based on assignments and grades. It's an intrinsic decision to read and write based on a sense of purpose and personal pleasure. Then when the assignments and grades stop, reading and writing continue.

10

Other Relationships That Affect Our School Lives

*T*here are days I would like to shut the classroom door and pretend the rest of the world doesn't exist. Inside Room 36 is a sense of well-being and purpose. We are right where we want to be, doing work of significance. Vivaldi's Guitar Concerto in D plays gently in the background. Kristen and Gabriella, stretched out side by side, are revising Kristen's poem. Charlie's pencil whisks across the paper as an idea jumps into his head. Andrew and Olivia peer into the rabbit's cage and sketch the class pet for their nonfiction project. Lost in thought, Mary draws an illustration of her latest writing. Campbell chews on the end of his pencil, crosses out a word, and chews again. We are a system in balance, complete unto ourselves.

But relationships beyond the classroom do impact our daily lives. How those beyond our walls perceive our work together contributes to my sense of who I am as a teacher. I feel valued or inadequate based on my relationships with parents, colleagues, and administrators. Unfortunately, there are times when I let myself pay more attention to the negative voices, the ones that wear me down. No matter how great my resolve to be thick-skinned, their comments vibrate through me like the fire alarm. Emotional support from other adults allows me to tackle each day with optimism and resolve. Without the support and the intellectual stimulation of colleagues, I'm a plant without the nutrients to grow. Please don't think me dependent and reliant on others for my self-esteem. I certainly try not to be. But like it or not, I am affected by how others treat me in the professional setting. Positive relationships provide a buffer, but negative relationships tarnish the day.

How do teachers find the required professional nourishment to give generously to children? Relationships that provide a flow of energy and information are a must—continuous communication that keeps the relationship with parents, colleagues, and administrators open and alive. This chapter looks at ways to build positive relationships with other adults in our school community.

RELATIONSHIPS WITH PARENTS

Advances in technology facilitate keeping in touch with parents. When I returned to the classroom a decade ago, there was one telephone in the faculty room. Receiving a call meant a fifty-yard sprint down the corridor. Now I have a phone in my room and contacting a parent is direct and convenient. Answering machines, voice mail, and beepers ensure they receive the call. They leave voice mail messages for me on my individual school number and know I will respond at the end of the day. Parents keep me informed about their children and issues that warrant attention.

Technology aids communication with parents, but it is my job to create a connection of respect and trust. The first week of school I send a note home offering conferences to parents who wish to meet with me. These short conversations jump-start my understanding of the child and parents realize I am sincere in my desire to know their child as fully as I can. Usually about seven or eight parents accept my invitation and our dialogue is worth the time. I plan one conference a day after school on days I don't have meetings.

The townwide conference weeks in November and April are valuable opportunities to learn more about each student. I try to listen with an open mind and heart. I'm Sherlock Holmes discovering the mysterious essence of each child. Talking to parents and hearing about the child of their heart nudges that child more fully into mine.

I paint a picture of the child in school, describing details rather than making judgments. The work in the portfolio substantiates my observations. My goal I take from Gandhi, "Speak the truth with love." Realism and optimism waltz together as we talk about their most precious asset. I take parent concerns seriously and jot notes as I listen. If I don't know the answer to a question, I promise to find out and I do. I want their support and don't mind doing my part to earn it.

Talking with parents about their child, whether on the phone or during a conference, is half of the communication equation. The other half is keeping them informed of events in school on a regular basis. They like to know what is going on and what is planned for the future. Weekly letters written by students serve this purpose, as well as a biweekly teacher newsletter telling of our work in each curriculum area and what's coming next.

Inviting parents into the classroom for exhibitions of work, performances, or informal learning times helps them understand more about life in the classroom. Some of my colleagues open their classrooms to parents every Friday for math games or to read with children. Others plan more extravagant events every month. However teachers find to include parents in the school day, it adds another link to the home-school connection.

A number of teachers appreciate the assistance of parent volunteers in the classroom. A brief training session prior to actual classroom participation prevents potential problems and increases the possibility of success. Parents help by typing student final drafts, reading with children, working with groups for special projects, sharing expertise or interests, videotaping, play rehearsals, and so on.

Surprises are fun when they arrive wrapped in colorful paper with a big, bright bow. Surprises are not fun when it is an upset father on voice mail worrying that Travis isn't being challenged in math. Misunderstandings often signal that a parent has received erroneous or inadequate information. Being proactive with parents means keeping them current about life in the classroom. Teaching children also means teaching their parents about the basics of life in my particular classroom, talking with them about the important rituals—morning meeting, birthday parties, and learning circle routines, as well as curriculum goals.

Students come with parents or guardians who are as unique and diverse as their children and they add or subtract to classroom life. When parents feel included and heard, their support contributes another source of energy. When they are discontent, it's a long winter. Keeping the lines of communication open and listening to parents with the same respect and acceptance we offer their children enables teachers to capitalize on the resources available when parents are partners in the learning endeavor.

RELATIONSHIPS WITH ADMINISTRATORS

One Friday night my husband and I went to see a movie and stopped at the local diner on the way home for a bite to eat. Sitting in a booth with her husband was a good friend and colleague. "Did you see a movie, too?" I asked.

"No," she said. "I've been at school preparing for my observation on Monday." She gave me a wry smile.

"You're kidding," I countered. "It's after nine."

"I want it to be perfect," she confided.

I walked on to the booth thinking about what it means to be a teacher. My friend is a careful planner and a fine teacher. But what felt disconcerting was the power her administrator has in her professional life—and if she's working until nine on a Friday night, her personal life. This is another reality of being a teacher.

Our relationship to our administrators impacts our daily teaching lives and even our after-hours lives. When we feel supported, understood, and valued, our lives in the classroom can flourish. When our teaching is questioned and challenged by an administrator, our confidence wanes and we second-guess ourselves. We imagine their doubts with every lesson and can no longer teach from our center. Like characters in the comics with balloon thoughts, we deplete our energy by listening to that negative voice in our heads as we interact with students. Administrators are often the only adults who observe teachers in action. Their advice may or may not be on target. Unless we have other avenues for learning and growing as professionals, we must rely on their perceptions.

The relationships I've most treasured with building principals over the years have been the ones where we spoke honestly and kindly. We confided in each other about the details of the students in my class and about our views of how I was doing to meet the needs of the students and parents. I knew the principals were just as committed to my success, the success of all the teachers, and the success of all the students. The bottom line was their integrity and humanity. They worked in service of the staff and the children. What an amazing example they set for all of us lucky enough to be in their charge.

I have heard horror stories about administrators who misuse their power and wreak havoc on the lives of teachers. Schedules that splinter the day, budgets that ignore teacher requests, emphasis on looking good that means superficial rules followed to the letter—there are so many ways to demean teachers and deaden life in school. They stop the energy from flowing freely. Communication is strictly transactional and usually one way—top down. Like wounded animals, teachers retreat to their classrooms and close the door. Some imitate the top-down power structure and pass it along to their students with rigid rules for every occasion.

It reminds me of *The Quarreling Book* by Charlotte Zolotow. Father is upset by something at work and speaks unkindly to Mother. Mother passes the bad feeling along by reprimanding her son. He in turn yells at his little sister, who shouts at the dog. The dog is unfazed by the criticism and joyfully chases his tail. The sister laughs at the dog and the spiral of quarreling reverses, each character receiving and passing on a feeling of happiness. Ah, if we were not all so vulnerable to the moods and attitudes of those around us.

Tenacious teachers break the chain of negativity. They keep their focus on knowing students well and on building an environment of trust and appreciation. They try to spare children the feeling of insecurity that permeates the adult culture in the building. Over time, however, the lack of emotional and intellectual support drives some gifted teachers from the classroom.

How do we build positive relationships with administrators? First, I must confess that I think some administrators are beyond redemption. Our energies are better spent finding other sources of support in our professional community rather than trying to reason with an unreasonable person. But when the administrator is a typically caring, overworked principal trying to attend to the mountains of details it takes to keep a building running smoothly, the key to a comfortable relationship is, again, communication. Here are a few tips for keeping your administrator informed of life in your classroom:

- Put a copy of your class newsletter in her mailbox. Even if she has no time to read it carefully, you are doing your part.
- Share concerns about students and parents in a quick note. She needs to be in the loop.
- Share success stories in a quick note.
- Invite her to bring a book and stop by for silent reading.
- Invite her to read a favorite book to the class.
- Invite her to join your morning meeting.
- Invite her to the classroom for informal performances, exhibitions, and celebrations.
- Invite her to have lunch with you and the class.
- Make a copy of informative articles and put them in her mailbox.
- Make a copy of notes you've taken at a conference and put them in her mailbox.

One of our professional responsibilities is to keep the principal in the information loop about the classroom. Some principals appreciate our efforts to keep them informed more than others. Email in my building has made it much easier to update the principal about classroom events. The better the principal and teacher know and understand each other, the more their relationship benefits the learning community.

RELATIONSHIPS WITH COLLEAGUES

I've taught in schools where collaboration and collegiality are the norm. Teachers thrive on sharing new ideas, successful lessons, and miserable failures. Doors stand open and teachers welcome other adults into their rooms. I've also taught in schools where privacy rules the day. Teachers guard their ideas and lessons like their supply of pencils. Questions about methodology or materials are viewed as prying. Conversations remain superficial and polite. As I look back at one particular school that echoed the silence of isolation, I realize the insecurity that accompanied the silence. Teachers felt threatened by fresh ideas and change. The unspoken status quo received their blessing.

In *The Courage to Teach,* Parker J. Palmer writes about how this affects our teaching:

> The growth of any craft depends on shared practice and honest dialogue among the people who do it. We grow by private trial and error, to be sure—but our willingness to try, and fail, as individuals is severely limited when we are not supported by a community that encourages such risks. When any function is privatized, the more likely outcome is that people will perform it conservatively, refusing to stray far from the silent consensus on what "works"—even when it clearly does not. (144)

The company of colleagues who support our zest to improve increases our commitment to being the best we can be.

Having experienced both ends and the middle of the collegiality continuum, I know what works best for me: teamwork and collaboration that offer an expanded view of teaching and learning. Inviting others, even those with differing opinions, to influence my thinking gives energy to what I do in the classroom. When I can be authentic and open with colleagues about my successes and failures, my life in the classroom is more real and less of a teacher role.

As I reflect on the ways teachers interact with colleagues, I envision this continuum:

- openly antagonistic—not even a hello in the hall
- quiet dislike—a head nod when passing
- masked dislike—pretense of camaraderie, with greetings
- passive acceptance—tolerance but no real support
- friendly interaction—chat about family, movies, the weather
- purposeful and animated interaction about teaching and learning

This last category moves beyond congeniality to collegiality, beyond celebrating birthdays and enjoying each other's company to learning and growing together. Conversations encompass professional issues and concerns that stimulate long thinking and sustained dialogue. Teacher study groups around topics, professional reading, or research questions assist teachers in their intellectual development and classroom practice. The emotional support of colleagues willing to dig deeper and longer supports the learning community just as Atlas holds up the world. Journeying and discovering together, teachers encourage and inspire one another.

In *Instruction for All Students*, Paula Rutherford says, "In most organizations things tend to get done because of *RELATIONSHIPS*, not through job description or formal roles" (1998, 269). Relationships promote or thwart the psychological health of a school. The quality of the human interaction determines how children, staff, and parents perceive the nature of the school community. Opportunities for formal and informal conversations on topics of importance make possible a higher, more meaningful level of communication.

Administrators in my district show their belief in a strong learning community by shortening the school day for a week in November and April so parents can meet with teachers. Grade-level days are scheduled every January so all classroom teachers from that grade in the district can gather and talk about ideas that work, new books they use with their readers and writers, areas of concern, and other topics decided by the teachers. Their ideas and enthusiasm enlivens the day as they talk candidly about life in their classrooms.

Principals understand the value of colleagues having time to talk with each other. They schedule the special subjects so each grade level has a regular time to meet each week. Teachers periodically attend workshops in the building and their classes are covered by substitutes. Some topics for workshops this year have been administering a Running Reading Record, essentials of a balanced literacy program, and learning about the next generation of the state mastery test. Rather than asking teachers to come to a meeting after school when most have already thought their last coherent thought, principals prove their support for professional growth by providing the time during the day for teachers to learn together.

But what if colleagues do not share a need for conversations and professional growth? What if the principal thinks staff development is a memo explaining the dress code? Fortunately, most teachers can be sustained with one other colleague who is a kindred spirit—someone who knows why picture day with seven-year-olds is so taxing, why another rainy day and another indoor recess could be the last straw, who will cheer when Charlie fills a page with writing, or listen to concerns about Claire's goal to collect every pencil in the room, store them in her desk, and insist she brought them from home. One other colleague can be the lifeline we need to keep ourselves going with style. I remember my early days of teaching when a dear friend down the hall made all the difference.

Collaboration is the norm where I now teach. I marvel at the professionalism and enthusiasm generated by teachers who talk earnestly and openly about their classroom practices, sharing ideas and materials as eagerly as young children share birthday cupcakes. And collaboration isn't just about comfort and support. Students benefit as well. "Teachers in successful schools are undeniably interdependent. Professionals working in concert produce cumulative effects in student learning," write Robert Garmston and Bruce Wellman in *The Adaptive School: A Sourcebook for Developing Collaborative Groups* (1999). "As more schools, districts, states, and provinces develop and attempt to implement clear standards and high expectations, the need for collaborative energy becomes increasingly clear" (15).

RELATIONSHIP TO SELF

As I was musing about relationships that impact the teaching day, I realized that how I am feeling, what I am thinking, my perspective on a particular day influences the way the day goes. When my energy flags, I'm aware of my inability to listen as closely or explain a concept in another way after the first four tries. I rally as best I can, but know I can do better and promise myself to do so tomorrow. I acknowledge with students that I'm running low, but will try to refuel with a good night's sleep.

I'm one of those drivers who doesn't stop for gas until the yellow warning light goes on and then I calculate I have at least another thirty miles before I need to panic. Too often I end up driving to the nearest station holding my breath. For years I ignored my own needs in a similar manner when the yellow light on my dashboard warned that I needed refueling. I had too many responsibilities and requirements. I had to override the stress and fatigue. I had learned to run on empty and most of the time I was too busy to notice. Plus, everyone else was in the same boat.

Perhaps it's the welcome wisdom that comes with age, but now I try not to do that to myself. I rejoice when I hear younger colleagues set limits and take time to care for themselves. As the flight attendant announces on takeoff, we must put our own oxygen mask on first and then assist others. This is not a recommendation to be selfish and unresponsive to the needs of others. It is a strong suggestion not to be unresponsive to the needs of our own bodies, minds, and spirits. Our bodies have ways of grabbing our attention when we ignore them for too long: colds, sore throats, headaches, stomach bugs, and so on.

How we feel as we greet our class each morning affects the day no matter how well we role-play pleasure. The relationship we have to ourselves, our own acceptance of who we are and how we're doing, enters into every interaction. We can try to fool ourselves that we mask our private concerns, but we know we are feeling under the weather or disheartened and that tugs at us during the day. By the time the buses with their noxious exhaust pull away from the building, we feel like we've inhaled their fumes all day; we are exhausted from our effort at duplicity.

Does this mean we stay home from school unless we're feeling one hundred per cent? Of course not. It does mean that we acknowledge our role in how the day progresses. Accepting our unintentional complicity in the script of the day provides a more panoramic view. We are less likely to wonder what's wrong with everyone else. The most powerful panacea I've found is staying in the moment. As I've learned to focus my attention and energy on the now, I am not drained by a duo–sound track in my mind. I have a clear channel for listening and responding. The end of the day I know I've worked hard, but it is a satisfying feeling.

One sunny day in October, I sat down to observe my class as they worked on a variety of activities. Everyone was engaged, happy, and productive. It was perfect! Why did it feel so right? Playfully, I jotted down what I sometimes inadvertently do to make the school day long and dreary. Here's my list:

TOP TEN WAYS TO HAVE A MISERABLE DAY AT SCHOOL

10. Decide that children should not act like children.
9. Focus on what children can't do or what they are doing wrong.
8. Demand behavior that runs counter to their developmental level.
7. Insist on having your way at all times.
6. Plan lessons that offer no choices and lack meaning.
5. Dwell on what is impossible to cover in the overwhelming curriculum.
4. Keep a mental list of the ways today's children are inadequate and deficient.
3. Harden your heart against overtures of affection from students or colleagues.
2. Drink several cups of coffee and ignore advice about exercise and a healthy diet.
1. Exhaust yourself staying up late doing schoolwork so that you feel resentful.

Relationships are about connectedness. From the time a child is small, the consequence for misbehavior is separation from the group: "Sit in the time-out chair" or "Go to your room." In school, the classic punishment for unacceptable behavior was to be sent to the hall or all the way to the principal's office. In the adult world, those who break the law must leave society and be incarcerated. The standard way to extract payment for ignoring the group norm has been separation and isolation.

If exclusion is a form of punishment, then inclusion must be a deeply felt human desire. Everyone does not need the same amount of participation and involvement to feel connected, but being disconnected strains the sense of well-being. When connectedness is viewed as a basic human need, the role of relationships in the classroom comes into even sharper focus. "Rules, routines, and procedures will count for little without also attending to the qualities of human relationships in the school" (Garmston and Wellman 1999, 21).

In *The Little Prince,* by Antoine de Saint-Exupery, the little prince learns a lesson about relationships. He tells the roses about his new friend, the fox: "He was only a fox like a hundred thousand other foxes. But I have made him my friend, and now he is unique in all the world" (70).

Vigorous relationships allow teachers to appreciate each child and children to appreciate each other. We are no longer just another person, but someone "unique in all the world." A personal relationship to reading and writing elevates our efforts to a higher plateau and literacy takes on greater significance in our lives. It informs and nourishes who we are. We value our own unique relationship to the written word. No one else writes from my experience and perspective. No one brings the same thoughts to a book as they read. The way I read and write is "unique in all the world."

Our world needs readers and writers. We need more individuals who understand point of view, perspective, and the value of collaboration—people who are comfortable with unanswered questions and ambiguities—people who willingly read to understand and write to explain—people who can vicariously enter the lives of others through stories and learn empathy and compassion.

Sometimes I worry that I am being unrealistic. Not all children will love books any more than all children will love to dance or solve math equations. But upon reflection, I change my mind. All children don't have to belong to the book of the month club as adults, but all children can learn to be confident, comfortable readers—readers who ask questions and think critically about the truth of what they read.

There are so many theories about why Johnny can't read or Jill hates to write. I believe Johnny and Jill can't read and don't write until that internal pilot light ignites—the light that creates the visual and sensory images, that activates prior knowledge, that gives meaning to the black marks on the page, that brings satisfaction and pride. It's this invisible beam of energy that establishes the visceral connection and links children to lifelong literacy. Meaningful relationships in the classroom—to the teacher, peers, reading and writing—are like candles that light the internal flame. And the miracle of a candle is that I can light others' without extinguishing my own.

CHILDREN MAKE THE WORLD A BETTER PLACE. THEIR DEVELOPING literacy is our hope and promise. As we help children create and fulfill their literacy dreams, the task of teachers is greater than choosing the right materials or teaching the right skills and strategies at the right time. For reading and writing to become a way of life for children, we must pay close attention to the relationships they have in the classroom: their relationship to their number one mentor, the teacher, the relationships they have to their fellow students, and the relationship they have to the stories they read and the stories they write. Therein lies the true potential for lifelong literacy.

Epilogue

Recently my husband and I drove into New York City. Our nephew Marc and his wife, Esther, had had a baby girl five days before. We wanted to see this first addition to our family in twenty years. She slept through our visit, her tiny profile content in slumber.

"Would it wake Hanna if I touched her hand?" I asked Esther.

"No," she said. "Go ahead. She feels so beautiful."

I stroked her delicate fingers in awe.

Esther reached down and lovingly stroked her cheek. "Touch her face. It feels so perfect."

I couldn't resist. Gently I ran my fingers from her perfect little ear to her perfect little chin. "Welcome, Hanna," I whispered.

As we walked quietly out of the bedroom, Esther asked, "She's beautiful, isn't she?" She closed the door behind us. "I never wanted to be one of those parents who thought her child was beautiful just because she was her child. I always thought I would be objective. If my baby looked funny, I'd accept it and love her anyway. I wouldn't insist that she was adorable."

"Oh, Esther," I said. "You're Hanna's mother. You're not supposed to be objective. You're supposed to think she's the most marvelous baby in the history of the world. And Hanna *is* 'unique in all the world.'"

"I used to listen to other parents talk about their babies and think I would be objective when I had mine," Esther added, smiling. "Well, I can't be objective. I love her!"

We laughed at how five days of motherhood could bring about this shift in her thinking.

"Parents are supposed to be subjective," I said, thinking the thought for the first time in quite that way. "It's your job to see Hanna through the eyes of

166

love and see more in her than anyone one else does. It's the reason she'll thrive."

I hugged Marc and Esther, my heart full. "Hanna chose great parents!" I said.

On the drive home I thought about beautiful, new baby Hanna and my conversation with Esther. Why does our society place so much weight on being objective? I remember having the same resolve before I had Sara. I would be realistic about her shortcomings. I wouldn't be blinded by love. What nonsense! Loving absolutely everything about her felt so glorious and right!

When we look at another person with objectivity, we have to distance ourselves from them—disconnect. We step back and imagine how others might perceive them and forget that there isn't one shared perception. When we see others subjectively, we bring all our understanding, affection, and acceptance into the picture. Love allows a nonjudgmental stance. We don't love this child *because* she is beautiful. We love this child because she *is*. Looking through the eyes of love we see things not visible to others. Like magic eye pictures, love allows us to see beyond the obvious.

In my classroom, I choose to look through the eyes of love. I don't want to be objective and distanced from children, from books we read together, from shared moments of laughter and learning. Objectivity filters out the humanness that makes teaching meaningful. It creates an arbitrary distance between teacher and children and weakens relationships that breathe joy and life into the school day. Being objective narrows our focus as we hunt for particular criteria. All that matters is what we are measuring. Everything else is of no consequence. There are times when objectivity is appropriate, but not in determining the value of a child.

I can never share that limited view of children and school. I welcome a more expansive view. Seeing Katie in my class in all her radiant potential, the way Mrs. Finkbinder saw me in second grade, is contrary to recent educational trends. After all, what counts are Katie's numbers on standardized tests. They decide if Katie and I are doing our jobs well.

But this measure of children is damaging to them and to my professional ethics. Yes, I want Katie to do well on the state mastery tests, but more important, I want Katie to do well in life. Doing my part means helping her discover the many aspects of who she is, her strengths, her areas for improvement—helping her learn to interact with others in a collaborative and productive way. First and foremost, my job is to ensure that Katie cares—about herself, other people, and her reading and writing. When Katie cares—when she is committed to her own progress and that of others—motivated from the inside out to learn and be the best she can be—she'll succeed.

And that means I must do no harm. I mustn't narrow Katie's literary world to required text, comprehension questions, blanks to fill, and random writing assignments that I grade in silence. To do no harm requires that I continually observe her relationships to gauge if she is prospering:

- What is Katie's attitude toward reading and writing?
- Is she enthusiastic about learning?
- Is she an aware reader and writer?
- How does she relate to me and to the other students?
- Do classmates respect her ideas and treat her like a class member of consequence?

Being vigilant about relationships for a room full of children may sound daunting, but with practice it becomes second nature. Many fine teachers attend to relationships every minute of the day without even realizing it. Their overriding desire to be respectful and of service to young students means their sixth sense monitors how children are feeling, what they are thinking, and their sense of connection to others and to what they're learning. When these teachers detect blips on their built-in radar screens, they make adjustments— often seeking student input. They map out a route that is responsive to interests, needs, and the learning styles of students.

The other day I was joking with colleagues about what can happen to teachers and administrators over time. We begin our career wearing an imaginary pair of glasses with plain lenses. We see clearly and delight in what we see. Each year the lenses alter slightly and it becomes harder and harder for us to see the world in focus. Eventually, the incorrect lenses give us a perpetual headache. We have to squint to see and our blurred vision subtly separates us from the world. Our decisions about children become knee-jerk and skewed. We've lost the bigger picture. Perhaps children unable to find school a natural and comfortable setting wear similar glasses that change through the years.

How do we keep ourselves and the children we teach from wearing the wrong glasses? By investing in relationships. When we are fascinated by children and find magic in reading and writing, those relationships imbue our days with a sense of wonder. The relationships we foster between children and their classmates and between children and their literacy enhances their ability to think, feel, and connect to the world in a considerate, thoughtful manner. Their vision of life in school remains clear and positive.

But to see these vital relationships, we must see with an open heart— willing to let relationships influence and transform us. Resilient relationships are the unexpected wisdom of a child, the smiling eyes of a young writer during group share, and the collective sigh when Charlotte, the spider, says "Good-bye." Like so many seemingly ordinary things, they add quality to our lives. When we take the time to notice, appreciate, and respect the integral role of relationships in the classroom, we enrich our lives and the lives of the children who journey toward lifelong literacy with us.

Bibliography

PROFESSIONAL REFERENCES

Albom, Mitch. 1997. *Tuesdays with Morrie: An Old Man, a Young Man, and Life's Greatest Lesson.* New York: Doubleday.

Ames, Louise Bates, and Carol Chase Haber. 1985. *Your Seven Year Old.* New York: Delacorte.

Atwell, Nancie. 1998. *In the Middle: New Understandings About Writing, Reading, and Learning.* (2nd ed.). Portsmouth, NH: Boynton/Cook.

Atwell, Nancie. Martha's Vineyard Summer Workshop: Writing in the Elementary School, July 1984.

Bayles, David, and Ted Orland. 1993. *Art and Fear: Observations on the Perils (and Rewards) of ARTMAKING.* Santa Barbara, CA: Capra Press.

Blue Cross Blue Shield of Connecticut. 1997. *Focus on Health* 8:2.

Caine, Renate Numela, and Geoffrey Caine. 1994. *Making Connections: Teaching and the Human Brain.* New York: Addison Wesley.

Calkins, Lucy McCormick. 1994. *The Art of Teaching Writing.* Portsmouth, NH: Heinemann.

Carlson, Richard, and Joseph Bailey. 1997. *Slowing Down to the Speed of Life: How to Create a More Peaceful, Simpler Life from the Inside Out.* New York: Harper-Collins.

Charney, Ruth Sidney. 1992. *Teaching Children to Care: Management in the Responsive Classroom.* Greenfield, MA: Northeast Foundation for Children.

Chopra, Deepak. "The Seven Spiritual Laws of Success." Fundraising television program for Public Broadcasting Systems.

Daniels, Harvey, and Marilyn Bizar. 1998. *Methods That Matter: Six Structures for Best Practice Classrooms.* York, ME: Stenhouse.

Duffy, Gerald G., and James V. Hoffman. 1999. "In Pursuit of an Illusion: The Flawed Search for a Perfect Method." *Reading Teacher* (September): 10–16.

Erikson, Erik. 1964. *Identity and the Life Cycle.* New York: Norton.

Ernst, Karen. 1994. *Picturing Learning: Artists and Writers in the Classroom.* Portsmouth, NH: Heinemann.

Fletcher, Ralph. 1993. *What a Writer Needs.* Portsmouth, NH: Heinemann.

———. 1996. *A Writer's Notebook: Unlocking the Writer Within You.* New York: Avon Books.

———. 1999. *Live Writing: Breathing Life into Your Words.* New York: Avon Books.

Fletcher, Ralph, and Joann Portalupi. 1998. *Craft Lessons: Teaching Writing K–8.* York, ME: Stenhouse.

Fountas, Irene, and Gay Su Pinnell. 1996. *Guided Reading: Good First Teaching for All Children.* Portsmouth, NH: Heinemann.

Fraser, Jane, and Donna Skolnick. 1994. *On Their Way: Celebrating Second Graders as They Read and Write.* Portsmouth, NH: Heinemann.

Gardner, Howard. 1993. *Multiple Intelligences: The Theory in Practice.* New York: HarperCollins.

———. "The Disciplined Mind." Speech given at the New York Public Library, 42nd Street branch, May 25, 1999.

Garmston, Robert, and Bruce Wellman. 1999. *The Adaptive School: A Sourcebook for Developing Collaborative Groups.* Norwood, MA: Christopher-Gordon.

Giacobbe, Mary Ellen. Martha's Vineyard Summer Workshop: Writing in the Elementary School, July 1984.

Golden, Arthur. 1998. *Memoirs of a Geisha.* New York: Alfred A. Knopf.

Goleman, Daniel. 1995. *Emotional Intelligence: Why It Can Matter More than IQ.* New York: Bantam Books.

Grafton, Sue. 1999. *"O" Is for Outlaw.* New York: Henry Holt and Company.

Graves, Donald H. 1983. *Writing: Teachers and Children at Work.* Portsmouth, NH: Heinemann.

———. 1994. *A Fresh Look at Writing.* Portsmouth, NH: Heinemann.

Hart, Leslie A. 1983. *Human Brain and Human Learning.* Oak Creek, AZ: Books for Educators.

Harwayne, Shelley. 1999. *Going Public: Priorities and Practice at the Manhatten New School.* Portsmouth, NH: Heinemann.

Healy, Jane. 1990. *Endangered Minds: Why Our Children Don't Think.* New York: Simon & Schuster.

Heard, Georgia. 1999. *Awakening the Heart.* Portsmouth, NH: Heinemann.

"How to Short-Circuit Negativity," *Prevention Magazine,* June 1997, 28.

Jacobs, Heidi Hays. "Mapping the Curriculum." Speech given at District Staff Development Day, Westport, CT, September 1992.

Jensen, Eric. 1996. *Brain-Based Learning*. Del Mar, CA: Turning Point Publishing.

Keene, Ellin Oliver, and Susan Zimmermann. 1997. *Mosaic of Thought*. Portsmouth, NH: Heinemann.

Lansing, Alfred. 1999. *Endurance*. (2nd ed.). New York: Carroll and Graf.

Lee, Blaine. 1997. *The Power Principle: Influence with Honor*. New York: Simon and Schuster.

Lindley, Daniel A. 1993. *This Rough Magic: The Life of Teaching*. Westport, CT: Bergin & Garvey.

———. "Finding the Energy, Renewing the Spirit." NCTE Convention, Nashville, TN, November 1998.

Moustafa, Margaret. 1997. *Beyond Traditional Phonics*. Portsmouth, NH: Heinemann.

Murray, Donald. Conference on Writing, University of New Hampshire, Durham, NH, October 1986.

Paley, Vivian Gussin. 1992. *You Can't Say You Can't Play*. Cambridge, MA: Harvard University Press.

Palmer, Parker J. 1998. *The Courage to Teach: Exploring the Inner Landscape of a Teacher's Life*. San Francisco, CA: Jossey-Bass.

Rutherford, Paula. 1998. *Instruction for All Students*. Bloomington, IN: Just ASK Publications, Inc.

Saphier, Jon, and Robert Gower. 1987. *The Skillful Teacher: Building Your Teaching Skills*. Carlisle, MA: Research for Better Teaching, Inc.

Sarason, Seymour B. 1982. *The Culture of the School and the Problem of Change*. Boston, MA: Allyn and Bacon, Inc.

Senge, Peter M. 1990. *The Fifth Discipline: The Art and Practice of the Learning Organization*. New York, NY: Doubleday.

Strachota, Bob. 1996. *On Their Side: Helping Children Take Charge of Their Learning*. Greenfield, MA: Northeast Foundation for Children.

Tompkins, Jane. 1996. *A Life in School*. Reading, MA: Perseus Books.

Vail, Priscilla L. 1994. *Emotion: The On/Off Switch for Learning*. New York: Modern Curriculum Press.

Wheatley, Margaret J. 1994. *Leadership and the New Science: Learning About Organization from an Orderly Universe*. San Francisco, CA: Berrett-Koehler Publishers, Inc.

Wood, Chip. 1994. *Yardsticks: Children in the Classroom Ages 4–12*. Greenfield, MA: Northeast Foundation for Children.

CHILDREN'S LITERATURE

Bulla, Clyde Robert. 1975. *Shoeshine Girl.* New York: HarperTrophy.

Cleary, Beverly. 1990. *The Mouse and the Motorcycle.* New York: Avon Books.

Clements, Andrew. 1996. *Frindle.* New York: Simon and Schuster.

Dahl, Roald. 1988. *Fantastic Mr. Fox.* New York: Puffin Books.

De Saint-Exupéry, Antoine. 1943. *The Little Prince.* (1988 ed.). New York: Harcourt Brace.

Fox, Mem. 1985. *Wilfred Gordon McDonald Partridge.* Brooklyn, NY: Kane/Miller.

Gardiner, John. 1988. *Stone Fox.* New York: HarperTrophy.

Giff, Patricia Reilly. 1980. *Next Year I'll Be Special.* New York: Delacorte.

Levine, Gail. 1997. *Ella Enchanted.* New York: HarperCollins Children's Books.

Marshall, James. 1988. *Fox on the Job.* New York: Dial Books for Young Readers.

Paterson, Katherine. 1989. *The Spying Heart: More Thoughts on Reading and Writing Books for Children.* New York: Lodestar.

Prelutsky, Jack. 1998. *The New Kid on the Block.* New York: Greenwillow Books.

Steig, William. 1985. *Solomon, the Rusty Nail.* New York: Farrar Straus and Giroux.

Winthrop, Elizabeth. 1985. *The Castle in the Attic.* New York: Bantam Doubleday Dell.

Zolotow, Charlotte. 1963. *The Quarreling Book.* New York: Harper and Row.